Abraham de Sola

The Sanatory Institutions of the Hebrews

Abraham de Sola

The Sanatory Institutions of the Hebrews

ISBN/EAN: 9783337418007

Printed in Europe, USA, Canada, Australia, Japan

Cover: Foto ©Thomas Meinert / pixelio.de

More available books at **www.hansebooks.com**

THE
SANATORY INSTITUTIONS

OF THE

HEBREWS

AS EXHIBITED IN THE

SCRIPTURES AND RABBINICAL W

AND AS BEARING UPON

MODERN SANATORY REGU

BY

ABRAHAM DE SOLA, L

PART I.

Montreal:
PRINTED BY JOHN LOVELL, AT HIS STEAM PRINTING ESTABLISHMENT
ST. NICHOLAS STREET,
1861.

SANATORY INSTITUTIONS

OF

THE HEBREWS.

~~~~~~~~~~~~~~~~

CHAPTER I.

INTRODUCTORY.

ONE of the strangest of all moral phenomena in the present day, is perhaps, presented in the comparatively trifling, nay, almost imperceptible, effects which the experience and teachings of ages have had in the legislative enactments and individual efforts of modern nations with reference to the all-important subject of health. Strange also is the fact, that although the principle of self-preservation, even in itself, should naturally incite communities, as well as individuals, to endeavour to profit by, and to act upon, teachings, always plentifully attainable, if duly sought, yet, by a most culpable negligence and apathy, more especially visible in large cities, have miasma and plague, malaria and consumption, been permitted to generate, and death to run riot, amongst those, who, but for the carelessness and cupidity of their fellow-men, might have attained an age almost reaching that of the patriarchs of old. Such procedure must not only be highly condemnable in the eyes of man, but necessarily sinful in the sight of God. For, as is his wont, the all-merciful and all-wise Creator has not left us without guidance in a matter which, next to the due care and health of our souls, it is most necessary for us to know. Thus, it never has been, as indeed it never can be, questioned, that the most ancient and, at the same time, most sacred treatises on the subject of a national and individual hygiene—the legislation of Moses son of Amram—contains the wisest and most valuable principles, recommendations, and enactments on the subject of health, which, though thousands of years have elapsed since their enunciation, do yet remain, like "all which proceedeth out of the mouth of theEternal," just as valuable and just as wise as when first revealed for the edification of the Hebrew people, and are, therefore, now, as then, fully worthy our most attentive and reverent consideration.

Among the Hebrews, who, under God, have preserved these enactments to the present day, it has ever been a golden maxim, "there are no riches can compare with health;"' and this principle is equally developed in their Post Biblical, as well as in their Biblical, jurisprudence, as it will be our endeavour to show in the following pages. The maxim appears also to have been in no small degree appreciated and acted upon by the ancient heathen nations, for, as we all know, their legislators not only passed laws calculated to secure an athletic, healthy race of men, who would best serve their respective states, but also for the healthfulness of these states themselves; and their orators and poets, as is also well-known, frequently called the attention of the people to the subject, in order that, being reminded in the words of Virgil,

> Noctes atque dies patet atri janua Ditis,
> Sed revocare gradum, superasque evadere ad auras,
> Hoc opus, hic labor est.†

they might thereby accord an universal and cheerful obedience to the laws. And even with respect to Christian nations, it is a question which, we think, cannot be so immediately decided in the affirmative, whether, in the first century of Christianity, they were less appreciative than their descendants are, in the nineteenth, of the truth conveyed in the saying of the old English moralists, that "there is but one way of coming into the world, but a thousand to go out of it," or whether they could parallel the atrocities which are daily revealed to us with reference to the impurity and adulteration of food, the state of city grave-yards, the noxious manufacturing processes carried on in densely populated neighbourhoods, and a thousand other evils calculated to undermine the public health. These, however, are questions we do not attempt to decide, but, leaving them for the consideration of others more competent to do so, we proceed to examine that branch of the general topic which we have selected as our own, and will endeavour to show what are the ideas and practice of that people to whom a code of sanatory laws was first revealed.

But it is proper to premise, that the Sanatory Institutions of the Hebrews are not to be looked for in the Bible only, though the grand principles, upon which they are based, have undoubtedly been borrowed

---

* אין עשר כבריאות · מבחר הפנינים

†Æneid lib. vi. (127) Thus rendered by Davidson, "Grim Pluto's gate stands open night and day; but to re-ascend from thence to the upper regions, this is a work, this a task indeed."

by them from, and credited by them to, the sacred volume. It is to that vast repertory of the national traditions, that well-known, but little understood, compilation, the Talmud, and to their later casuists, that we must turn, would we find and correctly estimate the multifarious, important, and highly interesting sanatory constitutions of a people who honoured these constitutions with a most scrupulous observance, not merely because they regarded them as mere matters of expediency, utility, or profit, but as the strict, unavoidable, and uncompromising requirements of their heaven-born religion. The pains and penalties following derilection or neglect—in some cases amounting even to excision—also tended, both in Biblical and Post Biblical times, to secure from the Hebrews a scrupulous observance of their sanatory laws. We are well aware, that some few, writing in an unfriendly spirit of the book in which they are contained, have condemned them as overloading men with useless ceremonies, which enter into every hour of his existence and make him the mere creature of ablutions and precautions. But it is very evident, that this objection must be pronounced quite futile, until it can be shown that a careful and strict attention to the promotion of health is at all condemnable, pernicious or unwise. By another class a further objection has been made to them, that, although their tendency may be good, yet is the minuteness of detail employed in the books of Hebrew jurisprudence highly objectionable, and not to be tolerated in the present refined state of society. But here it is also evident, that such an objection is utterly groundless, and could only be adduced but for a sinister purpose. For if they become objectionable and intolerable on this account, then equally objectionable and intolerable must we pronounce every medical book, tract, or treatise, from the days of Galen downwards; since it needs no very extensive knowledge of both classes of authors to decide that the former are clearly and indisputably more measured in their *modus scribendi* than the latter; notwithstanding which but few would recommend the suppression of valuable medical treatises on this account. The truth is, that, equally with any modern casuistic or scientific writers, the Jewish Doctors or Rabbis wrote for intelligent, considerate, truth-seeking men. They wrote neither for children, for fools, nor for blind zealots. And when they entered into details designed to promote the bodily, and consequently the mental, health of their people, they knew that they addressed men who would only consider themselves " a wise and discerning nation " accordingly as they respected the " statutes and judgments so righteous," upon which their teachers amplified—men, who, whatever their faults otherwise, could yet duly appreciate recommendations to purity, chastity, and sobriety, and could not only ostensibly, but actually and in reality, act up to them,

—men, whose cheeks would not mantle with the deceitful hues of a false
modesty when particularization of wholesome, sanatory and moral laws
were addressed to them in public, while, in private, they would, with brazen
brow and unblushing face, outrage every one of these laws, and yet loudly
proclaim a refined state of society, as, perhaps, is but too much the case
in our day. And that the Hebrew Sanatory Institutions, despite their
minuteness of detail, have proved to the nation neither hurtful to body
nor baneful to mind, is, we think, evident from various considerations. In
the first place, although there now flows in the veins of the Hebrews the
blood of the most ancient nation remaining on earth—the same blood which
once animated Abraham, Moses, David, and Isaiah,—although the stake
has destroyed of them its thousands, and the sword its tens of thousands—
although monarchs and legislators, from the days of Pharaoh downwards,
have passed enactments for their extermination, forbidding, as is the case
even in the present day, their obedience to one of the first laws of
nature*—although found in every country and clime, amidst the snows
and ice of a northern, and the burning sun of a southern, latitude,—and
although, at all periods of their history, subject to a thousand adverse and
destructive influences, yet do they remain a wondrous living problem,
the same *undeteriorated*, indestructible race, with the same characteristics
everywhere traceable among them, with an eye not less bright than
when it was called to witness the lightnings of Sinai's mount, and with
a step not less elastic than when it repaired to the Holy Temple which
God vouchsafed to make the place of His especial residence; in short,
with the same favourable, energetic, and high organization among the
men, and with the same instances of rare attractive beauty among the
women. Nor do we find them, in consequence of their sanatory regulations, more subject to diseases, or obnoxious to epidemics of all descriptions,
but the contrary; for it is undeniable that the mass of the nation, who are
duly observant of their dietary laws, are remarkably free from certain
classes of diseases, particularly those of the skin and the hypochondriac
regions; while, ever since attention has been given to the statistics of
epidemics, both in Europe and America, it has been announced as an
extraordinary fact, especially during the ravages of Asiatic cholera, that
proportionably, the Jewish community have remained in a remarkable
degree unscathed under these awful visitations.†

* In some parts of northern Europe the laws of the State permit only a certain
number of Jews to marry.
† During the fatal prevalence of Cholera in London, in 1849, the editor of a leading
paper thus writes: " It is a singular circumstance, that throughout the late awful
visitation, so few, if any, Jews, died of the Cholera in London, *although the majority
of them reside in districts where it committed great ravages.*" See also Thanksgiving
Sermon of the Rev. D. A. De Sola, of London, for 15th November, 1849. We
believe that the authenticated cases did not exceed two, and one of these, personally

These laws, too, have evidently not unfavourably affected their moral organization, for, let us search the calendar of crime of every country, and we shall be led to the conclusion that these same dietary and sanatary laws have had the effect of exempting them in a remarkable degree from that, to speak technically, plus-animalism, or preponderance of the animal organs and instincts, which has led in others to the commission of the most awful crimes. In vain we seek their names in the long list of those convicted of inveterate drunkenness, of midnight plundering and assassination, of fœticide, infanticide, of murder, and of other revolting and abominable crimes, which one dares not even think of or allude to. Of the correctness of this assertion it is easy to adduce evidence, but upon those who may feel disposed to doubt it, rests, as we imagine, the burden of proof to the contrary.

It would appear also that these laws have not had the effect of investing them with an inferior mental organization, for the attentive reader of history and observer of events, cannot but remain astonished at the immense, wondrous, influence they have exercised, and do even yet exercise upon the destinies of the world,*—in the present day,

known to us, was a gentleman of opulent circumstances, at Brighton, where he had gone for the advantages of sea-air.

*Although we might adduce abundant proof of the correctness of this statement also, yet do we attempt to satisfy our readers and ourself by simply quoting from one of the productions of the present Chancellor of the Exchequer of England. Mr. D'Israeli, in his Coningsby, thus writes : " The Saracen kingdoms were established. That fair and unrivalled civilization arose which preserved for Europe arts and letters, when Christendom was plunged in darkness. * * * * * During these halcyon centuries, it is difficult to distinguish the follower of Moses from the votary of Mahomet. Both alike of equally built palaces, gardens, and fountains ; filled equally the highest offices of the State ; contested in an extensive and enlightened commerce ; and rivalled each other in renowned universities." Sidonia, as a type, " was lord and master of the money market of the world, and of course virtually lord and master of everything else, and monarchs and ministers of all countries courted his advice, and were guided by his suggestions." * * * * * * " He had visited and examined the Hebrew communities of the world, * * * * * and perceived that the intellectual development was unimpaired." * * * * * " And at this moment, in spite of centuries, and tens of centuries of degradation, the Jewish mind exercises a vast influence on the affairs of Europe. I speak not of their laws which you still obey ; of the literature with which your minds are saturated ; but of the living Hebrew intellect. You never observe a great intellectual movement in Europe in which the Jews do not greatly participate." Mr. D'Israeli then, at length, shews how mighty revolutions are " entirely developed under the auspices of Jews," and mentions, as Jews, those who are or were professing Christians—at excelling in theology, Neander, Benary, Wehl ; in diplomacy, Arnim, Cancrin, Mendizabel ; in war, Soult, Massena. " What are all the schoolmen, Aquinas himself, to Maimonides ; and as for modern philosophy, all springs from Spinoza." In music, " the catalogue is too vast to enumerate ; enough for us that the three great creative minds, to whose exquisite inventions all nations at this moment yield— Rossini, Meyerbeer and Mendelsohn—are of Hebrew race." Pasta and Grisi also ! We cannot deny ourself the pleasure of quoting also from a lecture on the " Unity of the Races," delivered by our learned and esteemed friend, T. S. Hunt, Esq., of the Canada Geological Survey, as further evidencing the fact under notice, and as an excellent resumé of the above.

Mr. Hunt says: " We see the Children of Israel scattered over the face of the

more especially in the commercial and political world, though their influence and importance, religiously, as the ancient, preserved, and living witnesses of the Sinaic revelation, is by no means to be underrated. On this subject, however, it is not our province to dwell here, but we hasten to assure our readers that, in all we have said, we have not sought to assert that it is to their Sanatory Institution solely, that the Hebrews owe their preservation as a people. Far from this. In common with all believers in the Sacred volume, whether Christians or Jews, we witness the existence and preservation of Abraham's sons, and exclaim " the hand of the Eternal hath done this thing." Yes, we behold in it but the fulfilment of the predictions of their own lawgiver and prophets, the fulfilment of God's threats and promises to them. But in common with those believers, we are also impressed with the conviction that God frequently permits us to perceive and appreciate the means whereby He works out the end He proposes :—that He as frequently prefers simple and natural means for the accomplishment of His behests ; and that it is therefore quite permissible, after due inquiry to maintain, that the Sanatory Institutions of the Hebrews, have, under God, tended in a great measure to secure the present preserved and undeteriorated existence of the nation. To what extent they have done so it will of course be for the reader hereafter to decide. Believing, as we have already affirmed, that it is to a very great and important extent, we think no further introduction or apology necessary, ere we introduce them, as we proceed now to do, to these sanatory laws and constitutions themselves.

CHAPTER II.

THE PROHIBITION OF BLOOD.

THE Sanatory Institutions of the Hebrews may be considered as regarding—First, *Persons;*—Secondly, *Places ;* and Thirdly, *Things.* Our remarks will have reference to them under these three heads ; but we have considered it advisable to follow, as closely as possible, the order of

earth since eighteen centuries, without a country, yet finding a home in all ; scorned and trampled upon, yet often the power behind the throne directing the destinies of kings ; poor and abject, yet holding the golden keys of war and peace in Europe ; excelling in philosophy and in theology, in music and in art, in war and in statesmanship ; despised, yet ever powerful ; counted as aliens, yet, with their genealogies of forty centuries, looking down with scorn upon the aristocracy of Europe, which is but as of yesterday, when compared with their own proud lineage. The Hebrew people still preserves all its natural characteristics, and stands proud and imperishable before us to-day, the representative of the earliest ages of the world's history, and the evidence of the undying vigor of the pure Caucasian race."

the sacred volume, and, after due attention to its teachings, shall offer such illustrations afforded both by Christian and Jewish writers, as may be within our reach or memory, and necessary to do full justice to our subject. And first—*of the prohibition of blood.*

The first law best calculated to promote man's physical, as well as moral, perfection, is contained in the 28th verse of the first chapter of Genesis, and further expounded in the second chapter of the same book and in subsequent portions of the Sacred Writings. But we defer our remarks upon this law, until we reach the subsequent legislation of Moses thereon. In the seventh chapter of Genesis, we find the distinction made between " beasts that are clean " and " beasts that are unclean." This subject we also defer for after-notice, and proceed to examine the prohibition to eat blood, first expressed in the ninth chapter, third and fourth verses, of the book of Genesis, in the following terms, " Every moving thing that liveth shall be food for you, even as the green herb have I given you all. But flesh with the life (nefesh) thereof, *which is* the blood thereof, shall ye not eat." Such is the translation and interpretation given to this passage by the English authorised version,—an interpretation which we believe to be in strict accordance with its grammatical construction ; and such also is the interpretation of the great majority of commentators of all ages and countries. Here, it may, perhaps, be only necessary to cite those not generally attainable. " The prince of Jewish commentators," R. Solomon Jarchi, commonly known as Rashi, on the words " with the life thereof, which is the blood thereof," remarks, " God here prohibits to them (the tearing off and eating) the members of a living animal, and saith, as it were, to them, ' So long as the *life* (nefesh) *is in the blood,* thou shalt not eat the flesh.' " R. Abraham Aben Ezra on the same passage says, " The meaning of these words is this,—but the flesh *with its life, which is its blood,* shalt thou not eat, and this is in accordance with the reason (subsequently) given in Holy Writ, ' Thou shalt not eat the life with the flesh, for the life of all flesh is its blood, &c." ' Don Isaac Abarbanel has the following observations on this passage, he says : " And because in slaughtering animals for food, they might acquire cruel habits, God prohibited to them the eating of the members of a living animal––a custom which is certainly the height of cruelty. Therefore saith the text אך בשר בנפשו דמו לא תאכלו. The ב (beth) in בנפשו (benafsho) is used for עם (ngim—with) just as it is in ברכבו ובפרשיו (berichbo oobpharashav Ex. xv. 19,) &c. The text meaneth, therefore, And the flesh while yet its life (nefesh) is in it, the blood ye shall not eat of that flesh. Such is, doubtless, the right and proper exposition of this passage." Agreeably with his usual custom, before he proceeds to his exposition, Abarbanel states those questions he deems requiring particular notice, and here he seems ironically to ask, whether the blood be dependent upon the life, or the life upon the blood? " Surely," he exclaims, " the exposition of Haramban (*i. e.* R. Moses ben Nachman) which is ' but the flesh with its life *which is its blood, &c.*,' and which opinion makes the life (nefesh) to be identical with the blood, is a very erroneous one, and not for a moment to be entertained." It is with regret that we find ourselves unable to subjoin the exact language of Nachmanides, but must reserve our quotation from him, for an appendix. It seems, however, from Arbarbanel's own words, that he merely asserts what Rashi and Aben Ezra, nay, the sacred penman himself, seems to assert, viz., *the vitality of the blood;* and in such case, his opinion does not deserve censure, since it has met, during the last two centuries, with many deeply learned advocates, who, however, merely reiterate to a great extent, what Jewish exposition and tradition have maintained centuries before them.*

The learned Dr. Townley in his translation of a portion of the " Moreh Nebuchim" (Guide of the Perplexed) of Maimonides, says :—

" The doctrine of the vitality of the Blood, thus suggested by the Laws of Moses, does not appear to have been avowed by Medical Writers before A. D. 1628, the time of the celebrated Harvey, the discoverer, or the reviver, of the doctrine of the circulation of the blood, who, in his writings, maintained the opinion, but was never much followed, till Mr. Hunter, Professor of Anatomy in London, defended the hypothesis with much acuteness and strength of argument in his *Treatise on the Blood, Inflammation, &c.*, London, 1794, 4to. The arguments of Hunter were vigorously attacked by Professor Blumenbach, of Gottingen, who fancied he had gained a complete victory over the defenders of the vitality of the Blood. But his translator, Dr. Elliotson, in the notes he has added to the Professor's *Institutions of Physiology* (*Sect.* vi. *p. p.* 43, 44, London, 1817, 2nd ed. 8vo.,) thus sums up what he regards as the true state of the question :—' The great asserter of the life of the

---

* Hence the groundlessness of the following remarks in Wood's Mosaic History. It would appear that Mr. Wood had never studied the Talmud, or read Jewish commentators. We will not dwell here on the incongruity of his assertion that *Paul* (and therefore no doubt the Hebrews of that day) knew well and taught this doctrine, and yet, that (a somewhat gratuitous assumption we conceive) " it was 3600 years before it arrested the attention of any philosopher." Mr. Wood, perhaps, forgot that even before Paul, and long before Harvey or John Hunter, there were philosophers among the Jews who did direct attention to it. And yet Mr. Wood continues: " This is more surprising, as the nations in which philosophy flourished, were those which especially enjoyed the divine oracles in their respective languages." It is *yet more surprising* that Mr. Wood at " one fell swoop " taketh from Cæsar what belongeth to Cæsar and by this *ipse facto* assertion shows his utter want of information on the subject. We repeat, it would appear that Jewish tradition and commentary, like other small matters, had not troubled much the, in other respects, learned Mr. Wood. This, however, is *not* surprising.

blood is Mr. Hunter; and the mere adoption of the opinion by Mr. Hunter, would entitle it to the utmost respect from me, who find the most ardent and independent love of truth, and the genuine stamp of profound genius in every passage of his works. The freedom of the blood from putrefaction while circulating, and its inability to coagulate after death from arsenic, electricity, and lightning, may, like its inability to coagulate when mixed with bile, be simply chemical phenomena, independent of vitality. But its inability to coagulate after death from anger or a blow on the stomach, which deprive the muscles likewise of their usual stiffness ; its accelerated coagulation by means of heat, perhaps its diminished coagulation by the admixture of opium ; its earlier putridity when drawn from old, than from young, persons ; its freezing like eggs, frogs, snails, &c., more readily when once previously frozen (which may be supposed to have exhausted its powers) ; its directly becoming the solid organised substance of our bodies, while the food requires various intermediate changes, before it is capable of affording nutriment ; the organisation (probably to a great degree independent of the neighbouring parts) of lymph effused from the blood; and, finally, the formation of the genital fluids, one, at least, of which must be allowed by all, to be alive, from the blood itself, do appear to me, very strong arguments in favour of the life of the blood."*

Let us now see whether the sacred volume itself does not further support this doctrine of the vitality of the blood. With reference to the passage before us, in which, for the first time, it is apparently taught, we have already stated that we do not think the correctness of the rendering we have adopted can be disputed on grammatical grounds, and Abarbanel has, here, evidently, adopted his interpretation, an erroneous one as we conceive, from not having paid due attention to the accentuation and division of the proposition ; but to which, on other occasions, he attaches great importance.† Were there a disjunctive accent after the words " benafsho" (with its life,) then his interpretation would hold good; but, as it is a connective, it is, so far as accentuation has weight, plainly untenable ; while the commentaries above referred to, and to which we may also add the Targum of Onkelos, are clearly correct. But prior to entering upon an examination of the other passages

---

* " Blumenbach's Institutions of Physiolgoy," translated by Dr. Elliotson, Sect. vi. Notes p. p., 43, 44. Dr. Hunter's arguments may be found in an abridged form in Dr. A. Clark's Commentary on Levit. xvii. ii., and Encyc. Perth, art. *Blood.*

† It may be known to most of our readers that the Hebrew language possesses an all but perfect system of rhetorical accentuation, known as the Masoretic. The accents which are also musical, are capable of dividing a sentence into the smallest propositions, and may be considered as consisting of two classes, disjunctives and connectives. With the system, however, as presented in the Psalms and some other of the sacred writings, no one is fully conversant.

of Scripture bearing upon our subject, it may be proper to ascertain whether the word "nefesh," which is translated above, "life" has really such a signification. And this we can only ascertain by inquiring what are the meanings which some of the most eminent lexicographers have attached to the word.[*]

R. David Kinchi, in the first place, applies in his "Sepher Hashorashim," (Book of Roots), all the various significations, to *nefesh* which we find given, secondly, by Gesenius, which are : 1, breath ; 2, life, the vital principal in animal bodies, *anima*, which was supposed to reside in the breath ; 3, a living being, that which has life ; 4, the soul, spirit, as the seat of the volitions and affections, (the reader will be pleased, however, to compare what Parkhurst says, lower down, on this subject, under No. 4); 5, desire ; also, the object of desire ; 6, scent, fragrancy, odour. Buxtorf, Furst, David Levy, and Newman, give nearly all the same significations. Parkhurst has the following :—As a noun, it means, 1. A breathing frame, the body, which, by breathing, is sustained in life. See Gen. ix. 4, 5 ; Lev. xvii. 10—14, xxiv. 17, 18 ; Deut. xii. 23. From the above passages, he continues, it seems sufficiently evident not only that the animal body is called *nefesh*, but that this name is in a peculiar manner applied to that wonderful fluid, the blood, (Comp. Ps. cxli. 8., Isa. liii. 12,) whence we may safely conclude that the blood is that by which the animal doth in some sense *breathe*; that, agreeably to the opinion of many eminent naturalists,[†] it requires a constant *refreshment* or *reanimation* from the external air ; and that this is one of the great ends of respiration. Aristophanes, Nub. lin. 711, in like manner calls the blood "ψυχη και την ψυχην εκπινησι And they drink up my soul or life, *i. e.*, my blood." And Virgil applies the Latin *anima* to the same sense Æn. ix., lin. 349. "Purpuream vomit ille animam, he vomits forth his purple soul or life."[‡] The word means, 2ndly, adds Parkhurst, a living creature ; 3, the affections, desires, or appetites ; 4, *nefesh* has been supposed to signify the spiritual part of man, or what we commonly call his soul. I must for myself confess that I can find no passage where it hath undoubtedly this meaning. Gen. xxxv. 18; 1 Kings xvii. 21, 22 ; Ps. xvi.

* The Spanish Jewish translators, however, here (Gen. ix. 4,) render "nefesh" by the word *alma*, which, if we mistake not, always corresponds with "soul." Thus R. Menasseh ben Israel (*Humas ;* Amst. A.M. 5415) translates *Empero carne conu* alma *que es su sangre no commereys.* So also Dias and Fernandes (Bib. Esp. A. M. 5486, Amst.) Cassiodoro de Reyna, the earliest Christian Spanish translator, renders it *anima*, also meaning soul, but adds in a note, "*La sangre se dize ser el anima de la carne porque en ella reseden los espiritus vitales sensitiuos.*"

† See Tho. Bartholin, Anatom. p. 285 ; the Rev. William Jones' Physiological Disquisitions, p. 153; Dr. Crawford on Animal Heat, &c., p. 354, 2nd edit, and Encyclopædia Brittanica in AEROLOGY No. 89, &c., and in BLOOD No. 22, &c.

‡ See the Encyclopædia Brittanica in BLOOD No. 19, &c.

10, seem fairest for this signification. But may not *nefesh* in the three former passages be most properly rendered *breath*, and in the last a breathing or animal frame." Thus far Parkhurst; and we think we need now but look at the significations of *nefesh* as defined by the high authorities just quoted, to decide that we must translate it in Gen. ix. 4, as we have done, viz :—LIFE.

We proceed to enumerate all other passages having reference to the prohibition of blood, or to its vitality. In Leviticus, ch. iii., v. 17, blood is coupled with the *cheleb* (sacrificial fat or suet) as being everlastingly prohibited to the Israelites. In the 7th chapter of the same book, 26th and 27th verses, *excision* is denounced against the eater of blood ; " Moreover ye shall eat no manner of blood, *whether it be* of fowl or of beast, in any of your dwellings. Whatsoever soul *it be*, that eateth any manner of blood, even that soul shall be cut off from his people." At the 17th chapter, verse 10—15, the prohibition of blood is again repeated, and its vitality, apparently again taught. Verse 10, " And whatsoever man, &c.,* I will even set my face against that soul that eateth blood, &c. Verse 11, For the life of the flesh is in the blood, &c. ; Again in verse 12. In verse 14, For it is the life of all flesh, the blood of it is for the life thereof, therefore I said unto the children of Israel, ye shall eat the blood of no manner of flesh, for the life of all flesh is the blood thereof, whosoever eateth it shall be cut off."

Rashi remarks on this verse, " Its blood is here in place of its life, for the latter is dependent on the former." Again, " Life is the blood." And Aben Ezra says, " It has reference to the life, for it is known that the veins which proceed from the left side of the heart, are divided into two kinds, those of the blood, and those of the air, and these are (dependent upon each other) like the oil and flame of the lamp."† And here it becomes us to quote also what Abarbanel has written on this passage, in his elegant and elaborate commentary; since it will best serve to show our readers how the doctrine of the vitality of the blood long ago engaged the attention of the old Hebrew commentators, who, by the way, merely wrote in accordance with the received traditions of the Jewish Church.‡

Abarbanel says, " The illustrious Maimonides writes in his Moreh Nebuchim that the Chaldeans (Zabii and others,) although as a rule

---

*Mendelsohn says that the stranger or proselyte referred to in this verse, is the proselyte of righteousness, גר צדק notwithstanding which the Talmud, Treat. Sandrin, he affirms that the prohibition applies to others than the Israelites.

† From this passage it would appear Aben Ezra entertained an opinion, universally prevailing among the learned of his time, but which modern science and investigation have since exploded.

‡ See remarks on Woods' Mosaic History, note p. 10.

they rejected the use of blood as unclean, would yet eat of it when desirous of holding communion with evil spirits in order to know of matters future," (compare this remark of Maimonides with an illustration from Horace, which we shall have occasion presently to quote.) And therefore doth the law prohibit the eating of blood, and devote it to be poured out and sprinkled upon the altar. And therefore, too, doth the law proclaim, 'I will set my face against that soul that eateth blood,' as it does with reference to the giving of seed to Moloch, but which is not said with reference to any other precept. But Ramban objects to Maimonides, that the Scripture doth not so teach, but that the reason always assigned for the prohibition of blood, is that the life of all flesh is in the blood, &c., and that consequently, the prohibition is here on account of the life (of the blood,) and not because it was used for converse with evil spirits. Now, I cannot but be surprised that Maimonides doth not refer to the texts quoted by Ramban, teaching the vitality of the blood, as above, nor take notice of them, and that Ramban himself doth not refer to the passages Levit xvii. 7. 'And they shall no more offer their sacrifices unto devils, &c.,' which supports the opinion of Maimonides." It were needless to notice here the discussion into which Abarbanel enters on this subject, after these introductory remarks. Sufficient be it to state, that, with the Hebrew commentators, he, here, also maintains the life of the blood.

Thus far then we have three reasons assigned by the Jewish commentators for the prohibition of blood. The first is, that an end might be put to a kind of cannibalism, "which obtained," says the learned Dr. Townley, "even in the time of Noah, viz:—eating raw flesh, and especially eating the flesh of living animals, cut or torn from them, and devoured whilst reeking with the warm blood." Plutarch, in his *Discourse of eating flesh*, informs us, that it was customary in his time to run red-hot spits through the bodies of swine, and to stamp upon the udders of sows ready to farrow, to make their flesh more delicious ; and Herodotus (l. iv.) assures us, that the Scythians, from drinking the blood of their cattle, proceeded to drink the blood of their enemies. It is even affirmed that both in Ireland and the Islands and Highlands of Scotland, the drinking of the blood of live cattle is still continued, or has but recently been relinquished. Dr. Patrick Delaney says, "There is a practice sufficiently known to obtain among the poor of the kingdom of Ireland. It is customary with them to bleed their cattle for food in years of scarcity ;"' and the *Analytical Reviewers* observe : "It will scarcely appear credible at a future time, that at this day, towards the

---

* The Doctrine of Abstinence from Blood defended p. 124., note, London 1734. See also " Revelation examined with candour," vol. 2, p. 20, London 1732, 8vo.

close of the eighteenth century, in the Islands, and some parts of the Highlands [of Scotland,] the natives every spring or summer attack the bullocks with lances, that they may eat their blood, but prepared by fire."[*] The celebrated traveller, Bruce, relates with minuteness the scene which he witnessed near Axum, the ancient capital of Abyssinia, when the Abyssinian travellers, whom he overtook, seized the cow they were driving, threw it down, and cutting steaks from it, ate them raw, and then drove on the poor sufferer before them.[†] Sir John Carr states that "the natives of the sandy desert [between Memel and Koningsberg,] eat live eels dipped in salt, which they devour as they writhe with anguish round their hands."[‡] Major Denham also says that "an old hadgi named El Raschid, a native of Medina," who at different periods of his life "had been at Waday, and at Sennaar, described to him a people east of Waday, whose greatest luxury was feeding on raw meats cut from the animal while warm and full of blood.[§] And it is a well known fact, that the savage natives of New Zealand continue to quaff the blood of their enemies when taken in battle."

A second reason for the prohibition of blood is that assigned by Maimonides as referred to by Abarbanel as above, an authority respected as the highest in these matters by all theologians and bibical critics of all creeds.[||] We quote here, the passage in his "Moreh Nebuchim," to which Abarbanel apparently alludes, "Yet excision was denounced against some of them ; as *the eating of blood*, because in those times men were too apt to be led into a desire and precipitancy of eating it by a certain kind of idolatry, which was the chief cause why it was so strictly forbidden." And although Nachmanides, as noticed in our quotation from Abarbanel, refers the prohibition of blood to its vitality, yet is he also of opinion that its prohibition was grounded on the intent and design to suppress idolatrous customs and practices. He thus comments on Deut xii. 23. "They gathered together blood for the devils, their idol gods, and then came themselves and ate of that blood with them as being the devil's guests, and invited to eat at the table of devils, and so were joined in federal society with them, and by this kind of communion with devils, they were able to prophesy and foretel things

* Analytical Review, vol. 28, July, 1789. Retrospect of the Active World, p. 105.
† Bruce's Travels, vol. 3. p. 332—334, 8vo. See also some learned remarks by him on the present subject, vol. 4, p. 477—481, in which he designates Maimonides as "one of the most learned and sensible men that ever wrote upon the Scriptures," and an able defence of the statement of our author in Murray's Life of Bruce, p. 74, note.
‡ Carr's Northern Summer, or Travels round the Baltic in the year 1804, p. 436 London. 1805.
§ Denham and Clapperton's Travels and Discoveries in Northern and Central Africa, vol. 2, p. 36, note, London, 2nd edition, 1826, 8vo.
|| See Bruce as quoted above.

to come." These last words of R. Moses bar Nachman lead us to the
illustration from the writings of Horace, already referred to, when quoting a similar passage from Maimonides. It occurs in his Satires, 1st
book, Sat. 8.

> Vidi egomet nigrâ succinctam vadere pallâ
> Canidiam, pedibus nudis passoque capillo,
> Cum Saganâ majore ululantem.   Pallor utrasque
> Fecerat horrendas aspectu.   Scalpere terram
> Unguibus, et pullam divellere mordicùs agnam
> Cœperunt : cruor in fossam confusus, *ut inde*
> *Manes elicerent, animas responsa daturas.* *

Dr. Townley affords us further support and interesting illustration of
the assertion of Maimonides.   He says " the sacred books of the Hin-
doos exhibit traces of the same kind of worship formerly prevailing
amongst them.   In the Asiatic Researches, vol. v., is a translation of
the *Rudhiradhyaya* or Sanguinary Chapter" of the *Calica Puran,* by
W. C. Blaquiere, Esq., from which the following are extracts :—

" Birds, tortoises, alligators, fish, nine species of wild animals, buf-
falos, bulls, he-goats, ichneumons, wild boars, rhinoceroses, antelopes,
guanas, reindeer, lions, tigers, men, and *blood* drawn from the offerer's
own body, are looked upon as proper oblations to the goddess *Chandica,*
the *Bhairăvăs,* &c.   The pleasure which the goddess receives from an
oblation of blood of fish and tortoise, is of one month's duration, and
three, from that of a crocodile.   By the blood of the nine species of wild
animals, the goddess is satisfied nine months, and for that space of time
continues propitious to the offerer's welfare.—That of the lion, reindeer,
and the human species, produces pleasure which lasts a thousand years.
—The vessel in which the blood is to be presented, is to be according
to the circumstances of the offerer, of gold, silver, copper, brass, or
leaves sewed together, or of earth or of tutenague, or of any of the
species of wood used in sacrifices.   Let it not be presented in an iron
vessel, nor in one made of the hide of the animal, or of the bark of the
tree, nor in a pewter, tin, or leaden vessel.   Let it not be presented by

---

* Thus elegantly rendered by Francis:—
> Canidia with dishevell'd hair,
> (Black was her robe, her feet were bare)
> With Sagana, infernal dame !
> Her elder sister, hither came,
> With yellings dire they fill'd the place,
> And hideous pale was either's face.
> Soon with their nails they scrap'd the ground,
> And fill'd a magic trench profound,
> With a black lamb's thick streaming gore,
> Whose members with their teeth they tore,
> That they may charm the sprights to tell
> Some curious anecdotes from hell.

pouring it on the ground, or into any of the vessels used at other times for offering food to the deity. Human blood must always be presented in a metallic or earthen vessel, and never on any account in a vessel made of leaves, or similar substances." Thus far Mr. Blaquiere.

Further illustration is supplied by the profound Spencer, in his most valuable work, " De Legibus Hebræorum Ritualibus et Earum Rationabus,"† where he shows us how the heathen used blood, and sometimes, even human blood, by way of lustration. They imagined that the blood of their sacrifices was the favourite food of their demons. For this reason they were at the greatest pains to preserve it for them in some vessel, or when this was not at hand, in some hole in the ground. And then, while they ate the flesh, and the demon, as they imagined, drank the blood, they hereby not only declared themselves his votaries, and professed to hold communion with him, but considered themselves as having become purified.

Moses Lowman, in his " Rational of the Ritual of the Hebrew worship," well remarks on Leviticus xix, 26," ' Ye shall not eat anything with the blood' ought to be rendered at or before blood, and is an allusion to the idolatrous worship of demons by gathering blood together for them, as supposed their food, and coming themselves and eating part of it, whereby they were esteemed the demon's guests, and by this kind of communion with them, were supposed enabled to prophecy and foretell things to come—to have familiarity with these spirits, as to receive revelations and be inspired with the knowledge of secret things."

On an attentive and dispassionate ‡ perusal of the 17th chapter of Leviticus, already referred to, we think further strong support will be found

*The very opposite, it will be perceived, of the Mosaic Institution.

† Ed. Cantab. 1685. See also Shaw's History and Philosophy of Judaism. Part 1, ch. 1. Sec. 6.

[‡The following note was published i n the Canada Medical Journal, in accordance with the opinion and desire of some valued friends, and was intended as a reply to some criticisms on a former portion of our remarks. In deference to the same opinion and desire, and the note having been deemed of sufficient general interest and importance, it is now retained here.] We advisedly say "dispassionate," and assure our readers that here, as well as in every line we have yet written, we have earnestly sought to divest ourselves of all theological bias, being fully conscious that the character of our subject demanded this from us, and being quite mindful that our interpretation of the sacred volume would materially differ from that of many of our readers. And we do therefore humbly hope, that having sedulously endeavoured to avoid all of a dogmatic character in what we have hitherto advanced, we shall not be suspected of seeking covertly to propagate our peculiar views. We further hope, and indeed, are in the happy belief, that we are not living in a day when a believer in the divine inspiration and authority of the Holy Book—a descendant of those who, at the risk and expense of their lives, have preserved and transmitted this book to us —

for the opinion of Maimonides, that one of the reasons for the prohibition of blood was to put an end to idolatrous practices. The chapter commences with the command to both priests and people, that any making a meat sacrifice or " killing an ox, lamb, or goat, in or without the camp,

that we are not living in a day, when, because our interpretation of some portions of it may not be identical with that of the majority of our fellow-men, we therefore, may not open this blessed volume, to direct their attention, not to a matter of a dogmatic theological, or controversial tendency, but to examine with them what light it throws on a scientific question, which, though it has but for a comparatively recent period engaged men's attention, is nevertheless of the last moment to them. Nor are we willing to believe that we cannot occupy common ground, and that we have not been warranted in seeking to defend the sacred page from the insidious attacks of the scoffing and ignorant unbeliever, as we have endeavoured to do by adducing testimony of the highest order to the truth of the Scriptural teaching of the vitality of the blood. And although we may be charged with dwelling too long on a topic, not indispensable to our main subject, yet do we trust that our reason for so doing will be our excuse. The idea with us has been, who shall say that there are not those to-day, and that there will not be those to-morrow, ready to deny the Scriptural teaching on this point? It is reasonable to suppose that there are to be found those, less qualified to give an opinion than the learned Blumenbach, ready to do so. These remarks we have considered as being called for, by some of the reviews of our humble endeavours, which have appeared in the public press. And although we are of opinion that, as a rule, it is neither necessary nor wise to notice such,—we speak with all due respect, and with friendly and grateful feeling for the flattering manner in which all have spoken of us—yet, as they may convey the sentiments of some of our readers, we shall beg leave to take notice of some few. For the reasons already assigned in this note, more especially in that we have avoided all of a dogmatic character, we cannot agree with one writer, that any objection can attach to what we have advanced, because "it cannot be discussed in opposition to the writer's views, without raising theological questions which have nothing to do with science proper." We beg leave to repeat that we have avoided, and shall continue to avoid, all theology that is not common to Jew and Christian. If defence of a Scriptural assertion, bearing on a matter exclusively scientific, be likely to raise the theological questions to which this writer objects, then, we fear, that in opposition to his views, and at the risk of his future censure, we must persist in our past course. We cannot admit that the Scriptures, even if we do that theological questions, have nothing to do with science proper, for we believe that much valuable scientific information has originated from the Scriptures. On reference to what we have already written, we think we cannot be charged with obtruding our own views on the subject; we have merely, as a matter of information, shown our readers what has been advanced in sources, some attainable, some not generally attainable, to them. We of course feel incompetent to decide, as does our critic, whether we be a better pathologist or theologian. But we do feel ourself called upon to dissent entirely from his assertion, that " the human constitution must have changed very much in the course of the last few thousand years, if the rules of Leviticus are at all applicable now." We must not anticipate our subject, but we would ask, under what general heads may the laws of Leviticus be comprised? We can but answer, under those of caution abstinence, moderation, cleanliness, and purity; and therefore we can but add that the human constitution must have changed very much in the course of the last few thousand years, if the rules of Leviticus are not *quite* applicable now. We do not wish to speak disrespectfully of, or to underrate at all, the learned and accomplished Meade; but we do think that some further support and better illustrations of our critic's assertion should have been given, and is called for, than that adduced by him; which is simply, that " Meade (Medica Sacra, Lepra Morbus, p. 12) says that no trace is to be found in either Greek or Arabian authors, of leprosy in walls or garments; that the Hebrew doctors themselves admit that no such disease was known · in universo mundo,' excepting ' Sola Judea et solo populo Israelitico.'" We must remind the writer that others besides Meade have written on the leprosy; but admitting, to the

and not bringing them unto the door of the tabernacle of the congregation, to offer an offering unto the Lord before the tabernacle of the Lord, blood shall be imputed unto that man, * he hath shed blood, † and that man shall be cut off from among his people. V. 5. To the end that the children of Israel may bring their sacrifices which they offer in the open field unto the Lord unto the door of the tabernacle of the congregation, unto the priest, &c. V. 6. And the priest shall sprinkle the blood ‡ upon the altar of the Lord, &c. V. 7. That they may no more offer their sacrifices unto devils, after whom they have gone a whoring. § This shall be a statute for ever unto them throughout their

fullest extent, the correctness of Meade's assertion, does it follow because the disease has disappeared, that, therefore, the principles of treatment laid down in Leviticus are wrong and inapplicable now. We think the contrary to be the case, and that the disappearance of the disease, so to admit, speaks trumpet-tongued in favor of such principles of treatment. And if right and applicable then, why not now, when, as the writer himself admits, diseases are disappearing and *reappearing?* But further let us ask, whether the treatment prescribed in the case of contagious leprosy (for that the leprosy spoken of in Leviticus was contagious, there can be no doubt,) is not even now adopted in treating contagious diseases; and whether in small-pox, measles, putrid fevers and the like, separation and cleanliness, which is mainly the treatment prescribed in Leviticus, is not now, after an experience of thousands of years, prescribed in such cases of contagion. We are fully prepared to admit with the writer that " the nature of disease is continually changing, old diseases wearing out, and new ones springing up;" but as we have seen, from the example he himself adduces, an admission of this fact is not necessarily an admission that the principles of treatment which were efficient in preventing or removing diseases once, must be wrong or inapplicable now. In our introductory remarks, we observed that "the legislation of Moses, son of Amram, contains the wisest and most valuable principles, recommendations and enactments on the subject of health, which, though thousands of years have elapsed since their enunciation, do yet remain like ' all which proceedeth out of the mouth of the Eternal,' just as valuable, and just as wise, as when first revealed for the edification of the Hebrew people ; and are therefore, now, as then, fully worthy our most attentive and reverent consideration.' " Now, although we cannot flatter ourself that we have already " made our case good," as another critic has been pleased to say we have, yet do we not withdraw one iota of our expressions just quoted, and in taking leave of our critic, which we do with all kindly consideration and respect, we cannot but think, that after due consideration of the very little he has advanced in support of his position, the hygienic laws of Leviticus are good, are wise, are valuable, and are quite applicable to the human constitution even now.

* According to Rashi, he shall be considered as a man-slayer, and be responsible for the life of the animal sacrificed, contained in the blood which flowed in an improper place.

† This repetition Rashi thinks is intended to convey, that he who does not *sprinkle* the blood in the proper place is included in the condemnation of the text.

‡ " The blood of the victim was received by the priest in a vessel for that purpose called פרים and was scattered at the foot, and on the sides of the altar. The blood of sin offerings was likewise placed upon the horns of the altar, and if they were offered for the whole people or for the high priest, it was sprinkled towards the veil of the Holy of Holies ; and on the day of propitiation on the lid of the ark, and likewise on the floor before the ark. The blood was also placed on the horns of the altar of incense ; a ceremony which was termed by the more ancient Jews כפר *expiation*, but by those of later times נתינה a *gift*. Lev. 4, 7. 8 ; 15, 16. Zech 8, 15 ; Num. 18. 17." *Jahn.*

§ Aben Ezra well remarks, that all who seek and serve the devil-gods or idols may most fitly be said to be faithless to the true God to whom they are betrothed by covenant. Can any one suppose, he asks, that there can exist any other cause of good or evil, but the Holy One, blessed be He !

generations." The intention of these words, we think, cannot be mistaken. It is evidently to secure the direction of divine worship to its proper object, and to put an end to idolatrous practices. In verses 8 and 9, the same directions and penalties are laid down with reference to burnt offerings or sacrifices. And then (v. 10) evidently and unquestionably, in the same connexion, follows the prohibition and penalty against eating blood ; *all blood* is the expression used by the text, because, as Rashi aptly remarks, " the principle being laid down in verse 11, that it is the blood that maketh an atonement for the life (nefesh,) and as the Israelites might conclude that reference here was only made to the blood of animals consecrated for sacrifice, therefore the text explicitly states *all blood*." Next follows as we conceive another reason why blood should not be eaten, viz. ; " for the life of the flesh is in the blood," V. 11. And I have given it you upon the altar to make atonement for your life, (nefesh,) for the blood maketh an atonement for the life,* (nefesh.) V. 12. Therefore have I said unto the children of Israel, no soul of you shall eat blood, neither shall any stranger that sojourneth among you † eat blood, &c. In verse 13 ,the blood of beasts or fowl that may be eaten, is directed to be *poured on the ground* and to be *covered with dust ;* another preventitive of idolatrous practices. In verse 16, we are again told that blood is the life of the flesh, the blood of it is for the " nefesh " or life thereof, and that hence is the prohibition.

. Further support to the opinion of Maimonides may be deduced from Levit. xix. 26—"Ye shall not eat anything with the blood, neither shall ye use enchantments nor observe times." The connexion of the one prohibition with the latter having reference to idolatrous practices, we take to be very significant, especially as the following verse has evident reference to the same subject. In Duet. ch. xii, v. 16, the prohibition to eat blood is repeated, and the command to " pour it upon the ground like water ;" and at verse 27, the blood of sacrifices is to be poured upon the altar of God. Again at chap. xv, v. 23. The incident in the first book of Samuel, ch. 14, v. 32-34, would tend to show that the people of Israel considered the majesty of heaven peculiarly outraged by the eating of blood

---

* On this passage Rashi remarks, " For all healthfulness of life depends on the blood, therefore, saith God. I have appointed that ye pour the blood on my altar, since by bringing me the life-blood of beasts, you show you have considered your own life has been forfeited by you, and you bring one life, which I have already permitted you to take. in place of another." We do not use the exact words of Rashi. but endeavour briefly to give his meaning.

† Since we find here the prohibition is extended to proselytes also, we may perhaps see an additional reason in favour of the opinion of Maimonides. The proselytes were forbidden it, as they were idolatry, since their example might prove contagious. Hence, as Aben Ezra remarks, the command to cover the blood in v. 13, also applies to them.

there spoken of. King David appears clearly to point out the connexion between the prohibition of blood-eating and the idolatrous practices of the heathen. He says in the 16th Psalm, v. 4, their sorrows shall be multiplied that hasten after another god, *their drink offerings of blood* will I not offer, &c." We will not seek for further illustrations, but trust that sufficient have been adduced to show that the opinion entertained by Maimonides is not without scriptural warrant.

The third reason for the prohibition of blood, viz, because of its vitality, must have been anticipated by a perusal of the scripture passages already quoted. There is but one passage more, to which we would more fully refer here. It is Deut., ch. 12., v. 23, " Only be sure (Heb. Be strong) that thou eat not the blood, for the blood is the life (nefesh)'; and thou mayest not eat the life (nefesh) with the flesh.

[For the origin and appearance of the following note, see page 17. note.]
* As involving a question of general interest, and bearing immediately on our subject, we would, briefly as possible, notice here some remarks made by a critic in a sister city on our observations on the Hebrew word *nefesh.* The writer says that we " endeavour to show that the Hebrew word " *nefesh*" signifies not so much the spirit, or seat of the volitions and affections, as life, mere animal life, and that the name is in a peculiar manner applied to that wonderful fluid, the blood, &c." Now, " with the utmost deference to the learned writer we beg to be permitted to state. that" after reading over our observations, we cannot find that we have written what he thinks we have. We gave no opinion as to what is *always* the meaning of " *nefesh*" but simply quoted from authorities of the very highest order, to show that we were quite warranted in translating it *life* in the *ninth chapter 4th verse of Genesis.* We did not think it at all necessary to enter too fully into the vast field of philological dissertation, especially, too, when it might lead us into the still vaster neld of theological disputation. But as our attention has been called to the matter, we think it right to say that our opinion really is that נפש (nefesh) never means soul, as our critic seems to think, but that the word נשמה (neshama) does. And this conclusion we form from no theological leaning. That great Christian Hebrew scholar, Parkhurst, who can by no means be accused of having or showing any great respect for Rabbinical or Jewish interpretation, bears us out in our conviction, that " there is no passage in which it hath undoubtedly this meaning, but in those which seem fairest for this interpretation, it means a breathing, or animal frame." See our quotation from him. There is nothing at all spiritual in the root which is נפש (nafash) to respire, take breath, without reference to the soul. A sufficient confutation of contrary opinion is contained in the very passage quoted in support by our critic. " The Lord God formed man of the dust of the ground, and breathed (ויפח vayipach) into his nostrils a living soul, נשמת חיים (nishmat chayim) in regimen, literally, a soul of life, just as the law is elsewhere said to be a עץ חיים (a tree of life, ngets chayim.) or living tree. Observe the word employed in this passage, which in common with most Jewish and Christian commentators, we understand as teaching the infusion by God in man, not only of his life, animal life, but his spiritual life, too, indicated by the word "neshamah." We particularly observe that "nefesh" is not here used, but "neshamah" The text concludes, " and Man became נפש חיה (lenefesh chaya.) a living being ; i e., the dust shaped by the hand of Omnipotence, became by the divine agency, a man, a living being ; a rational one, too, the text teaches us, since we find the just-shaped earthly mass received a " neshamah" or soul. We presume none will venture to deny that " nefesh" does not very frequently signify in the Scriptures, a person, an individual. If there should be any, notwithstanding that every Hebrew lexicon of any character would prove their error, we will refer them to a dozen passages occurring in Leviticus alone, where it can mean nothing else, to wit, ch., 4, v., 2 ; 4, 27 ; 5, 2 ; 5, 4 ; 5, 15 ; 5, 17 ; 5, 21 ; 7, 27 ; 17, 12 ; 17, 15 ; 22. 6 ; 22, 11. Nevertheless upon the strength of the passage from Genesis just quoted, the assertion is made that "nefesh"

Thou shalt not eat it, thou shalt pour it upon the earth as water. *Thou shalt not eat it*, that it may go well with thee and with thy children after thee, when thou shalt do that which is right in the sight of the Lord." The most emphatic form of expression, it will be perceived, is here used with reference to the prohibition ; the reason of it again assigned, being because of its vitality.

does not signify life, and is not therefore identical with the blood. We never said, as our critic appears to have understood us, that "nefesh" life is identical with "dam" blood. We think, on the contrary, the words convey two very distinct ideas, notwithstanding our belief, that life has connection with the blood ; therefore, he has formed his conclusion rather hastily and unwarrantably. We concur with the following passage from the writer, except in one small, but important. particular. upon which we shall remark within brackets. "Until the breath of life was breathed into man's face, the "nefesh" was dead. [We would rather say it was *the body* that was dead especially since the writer joins with us in the belief that the animating principle was directly bestowed by God, and that then man became a living being : he adds] the soul wanted animation. [To say the least of it. we think that this expression of our critic involves some little self-contradiction. We again repeat it was *the body* that wanted animation. not the soul ; and the contradictoriness of our critic's assertion is shown in this ; he first asserts that "nefesh" means soul, and then that the *soul wanted animation !* Now to find such an assertion as the latter made by a religionist, a reverent Scripture reader, and a scholar, all which our critic evidently is, we think an amazing thing. Surely he shares the belief that man's soul is an emanation from God, is immortal, and consequently, that it never was dead in Adam, but that from the moment it was breathed in him, from that moment it lived —ay—and lives even now, while we write. and while he reads. The writer continues, "True, Mr. De Sola may allege that this breathing into the face or nostrils has reference to the first circulating of the blood, and suggested the practice adopted in cases of suspended animation from drowning, or other modes of suffocation. [We have already given our ideas on this subject.] Perhaps so, but it shows that there are in the Hebrew, distinct words signifying the life, the soul, and the blood, things quite distinct, however closely related to each other they may be. [We agree here *in toto* with the writer, and hence our humble attempt above to show that what meant soul did not mean life, as according to his views of "nefesh." it must needs do.]—And more than that with respect to the reason for the prohibition of the eating of blood, Mr. De Sola is labouring under a mistake. [We can scarcely consider this remark written with that fairness which it is due to state, our critic has throughout displayed. We have as yet, merely given, not as our own opinion, but as the opinion of celebrated Christian and Jewish authorities, *some* of the reasons assigned for the prohibition. Had our remarks on the prohibition of blood been at end, we might then be justly charged with overlooking those reasons of most import, and more immediately having reference to the Sanatory Institutions of the Hebrews. As will be presently seen, we have by no means overlooked these reasons. Our critic continues,] David did not, when he said, "elecha adonai nafshi essa," unto Thee, O Lord I lift my "nefesh," surely intimate that he offered only his life's blood as a sacrifice to the Lord." Thus far our critic. We think that David as an Israelite might, and really did, use the word as signifying life. And without reference to that theological dogma involved by raising this question. and upon which the writer and ourself necessarily differ, we may be permitted to say that David may convey that in this word he offers to God all he could, and which we should all offer him—the undivided earnest. devotion of our "nefesh," that is of our life—a mode of expression, as common to the Hebrew, as to the English, language, conveying all the functions, the source, and energies of life. But as we are disqualified here, from entering into questions of a dogmatic controversial character, we must beg to take a friendly leave of our critic, and in so doing, must apologise to our readers for detaining them so long from our main subject, which we have done only because we have been assured they were concerned in the important questions this note involves.

The foregoing reasons assigned for the prohibition of blood-eating may be considered as the *moral*. But it has been traditionally held by the Hebrew people that the prohibition of blood is also a *Sanatory law*, in other words that blood-eating is forbidden on account of the baneful effects of the practice, physically. And we hold that sufficient intimation of this is given in the sacred volume itself, irrespective of what may be contained on the subject in the Talmud and other authoritative sources. That the practice is really a bad one in a sanatory point of view, we think is shown, 1st, by the Scriptures; 2ndly, by the commentators; and, 3rdly, by other authorities.

1. *The effects of blood eating are shown to be physically bad by the Scriptures.* We shall quote a few passages only, thinking they are sufficient to show that the fact is clearly intimated by inspiration. It is *clearly conveyed in the whole of the ceremonial law*, which, we presume it will not be denied, was intended to promote the physical as well as the moral well-being of the Hebrews. The practice is spoken of as one that defileth. And in the prophets it is also spoken of as a practice of baneful effects; one passage will perhaps suffice. In the book of the prophet Isaiah ch. 49, v. 26, God in denouncing his heavy judgments against those who oppress Israel, proclaims the following as their awful punishment, " And I will feed them that oppress thee with their own flesh [what would be the fearful effects of " eating their own flesh" must be known to all ; in the same connexion the text immediately adds] and they shall be drunken with their own blood as with sweet (or new) wine." Here the text we think clearly and aptly illustrates the effects of blood eating, which, as has been indisputably shown by experience, has really the same effect, when taken in quantity, as wine; for it both maddens and stupifies, and this, whether human blood, or the blood of beasts. In the same way speak Jeremiah, Ezekiel and the other prophets. And with inclination and opportunity, it would perhaps be no difficult matter to show that among the earliest Christian churches they abstained as " necessary things" from " things strangled and from blood," because they considered the command, tending not only to promote the health of their soul, but of their body too.

2. *The effects of blood eating are shown to be physically bad by the commentators.* The Hebrew writers constantly and earnestly inculcate a loathing, we might rather say an abhorrence, of the practice, which they regard as destructive both to body and mind. They regard blood as a most unwholesome article of diet, and as inducing a gross, plethoric, and vitiated state of body Some fifteen centuries back, the Talmud, in its concise but emphatic manner, proclaimed—and it then merely repeated old teachings in Israel בריש כל מרעין אנא דם—(the main cause

of all disease is blood.) ˙ Again, in the same passage דם אנא מותא כל בריש —(the main cause of all death is blood.) And again דם רבה שחין רבה —(much blood, much scurvy.)† But as we shall presently have occasion to call the reader's attention to those constitutions of the Jewish ritual having especial reference to this subject, and as our limits therefore will forbid our multiplying quotations, here we think it proper to state at once those objections with which Christian commentators have supplied us. Our limits will compel us to brevity here also, wherefore we can do no better than to present what we may regard as a digest of Christian commentary supplied us by the learned Dr. Townley. A further reason we have for doing this is to show that in the three positions he, we think very correctly, assumes, and advances as the results of modern investigation and science, Dr. T. has been anticipated by Hebrew writers at an age almost as early as the introduction of Christianity.‡ This we may see by comparing the Talmudic quotations above with Dr. Townley's three propositions.

The first Talmudic axiom quoted, was, that " the main cause of all disease is blood," and we maintain that is to the eating of blood this remark refers. The observations of Dr. Townley will appear to the candid reader to be nothing more than illustration and commentary on these axioms, though doubtless involuntarily so on his part, for we may be permitted to suppose that the Doctor, without any imputation on his Rabbinical learning, which seems to be of no mean order, did not know, or perhaps did not recollect, these Talmudic passages. We say, then, that Dr. Townley observes—and *not* with reference to the first of the Talmudic axioms we have quoted, though we request the reader to compare ; " the blood being highly *alkalescent*, especially in hot climates, is subject to speedy putrefaction ; and, consequently, that flesh will be most wholesome and best answer the purposes of life and health, from which the blood has been drained, and will preserve its suitableness for food the longest.

Our second Talmudic quotation was, " the main cause of all disease is blood," Dr. Townley remarks : " 2nd. Blood affords a very gross nutriment, and is very difficult of digestion, and in some cases it is actually dangerous to drink it : for if taken warm and in large quantities, it may

---

* Batra f. 58. b.   † Bechor. f. 44. b.

‡ It may be known to the reader that there are two Talmuds in use among the Jews. The 1st, the *Talmood Yerushalmi* or Jerusalem Talmud, was compiled in the year 230, according to some in the year 300, of the Christian era. This, however, is not so much in use, and does not contain so many legal decisions as the 2nd, the *Talmood Babli* or Babylonian Talmud, completed about the year 500. It need scarcely be remarked that the Talmud contains traditions which were generally acknowledged by Jews, and were ancient even at the time of their compilation.

prove fatal, particularly bull's blood, which was given, with this view, to criminals by the Greeks, " its extreme viscidity rendering it totally indigestible by the powers of the human stomach." Valerius Maximus (lib. v. c. 6.) ascribes the death of Themistocles to his having purposely drunk a bowl of ox blood during a sacrifice, in order to avoid subjecting his country, Greece, to the King of Persia. It is true, the blood of animals does not always produce similar effects, but this may be owing rather to the smallness of the quantity taken, than to its not being injurious in its nature ; or its malignity may be partially counteracted by the other dietetic substances with which it may be eaten.*

The third Talmudic axiom was, " Much blood, much scurvy". Dr. Townley says " 3rd. Those nations which feed largely upon flesh, are observed to be remarkably subject to *scorbutic diseases ;* and if physicians be right in ascribing such tendency to animal food in general when freely eaten, especially in the hotter climates, it must be acknowledged that the grosser and more indigestible juices of such food must have the greatest tendency to produce such injurious consequences ; and blood as the grossest of all animal juices, be the most inimical to health and soundness.†
To abstain therefore from all meat, from which the blood has not been drained, from whatever cause the blood has been retained in the animal, whether purposely, by strangling or otherwise, must be much more conducive to health then by yielding to a luxurious and vitiated taste, and adopting a contrary practice.

3. *The effects of blood eating are shown to be physically bad by other authorities.* The Abbé Fleury (Mœurs des Israelites) says, the Hebrews " were forbidden to eat blood or fat, both are *hard of digestion :* and though strong working people, as the Israelites, might find less inconvenience from it than others, it was better to provide wholesome food for them, since it was a matter of option." Dr. Townley says, " the divine Being enjoined that animals destined for food should be killed with the greatest possible despatch, their blood be poured upon the ground, and the eating of blood religiously avoided ; and still more deservedly prohibits such sanguinary food from *its baneful influence upon the dispositions* of those whose vitiated appetites or brutal superstitions led them to indulge in gross and bloody repasts." For as has been remarked " all animals that feed upon blood, are observed to be much more *furious* than others. ‡ Bryson (Voyage, p. 77.) tells us that the men by eating what

---

* Dr. A. Clarke's commentary on Levit. xvii. 11.—Michaelis's Commentaries on the Laws of Moses, vol. 3. art. 206, p. 252.—Revelation examined with Candour vol .2. 23. Encyc. Perth., article *Blood.*

† Revelation examined with Candour," *ut sup.*

‡ Delaney's " Revelation examined with Candour," vol. ii., p. 21.

they found raw, *became little better than cannibals.* * Further illustration of this fact we think may be found in Alexander Henry's Travels through Canada and the Indian Territories. In that work it is stated that " man-eating was then, and always had been, practised among the Indian nations, for the purpose of giving them courage to attack, (in other words to *shed blood.*) and resolution to die, (in other words *a brutish indifference to death.* † This extract (for which we are indebted to Priest's American Antiquities,) shows us that *savages* at least could estimate the value of blood eating. That ultimately it may insidiously gain ground, and advance until men indeed *become little better than cannibals*, we think is shown in the case referred to by Baron Humboldt in his personal narrative, he says that " in Egypt" once, as our readers will please recollect, the centre of refinement; here, "in the 13th century, five or six hundred years ago, the habit of eating human flesh pervaded all classes of society. Extraordinary snares were spread, for physicians in particular. They were called to attend persons who pretended to be sick, but who were only hungry, and it was not in order to be consulted, but to be devoured." Michaelis says, " drinking of blood is certainly not a becoming ceremony in religious worship. It is *not a very refined custom*, and if often repeated, it might probably *habituate a people to cruelty and make them unfeeling with regard to blood;* and certainly religion should not give, nor even have the appearance of giving, any such direction to the manners of a nation."‡

Having thus seen that the practice of blood-eating is one by no means commendable, or conducive to *mens sana in corpore sano* we proceed now to detail the various requirements and enactments laid down in the Jewish ritual code—the Talmud, Maimonides and other rabbinical authorities—having reference to the slaughtering of animals, and abstinence from blood; since they will best show with what religious strictness and sedulous care Israelites are required to (and in fact do now really) exhibit to remove the possibility of their eating prohibited blood. We ask the reader's indulgence in that, hereby, we shall have to extend considerably our remarks on this one sanatory Institution of the Hebrews; but we think it right so to do, and shall, on other occasions when we may have to elaborate, inasmuch as in our introductory remarks we said that after due attention to the sacred

---

* Fergus's Short Account of the Laws and Institutions of Moses, p. 99, note. Dunfermline 1810, 8vo. c. 8. See also Marshami, Chronicon, sec ix, p. 185. Lipsiæ, 1676, 4to.

† Medical Repository, vol. 14, pp. 261, 262.

‡ Michaelis's Commentaries on the Laws of Moses; vol. iii., p. 252.

text we should "offer such illustrations afforded both by Christian and Jewish writers as may be within our reach or memory, and necessary to do full justice to our subject." And since we consider that the enactments alluded to above, should be noticed as being *intimately* connected therewith : and that to the inqùiring English reader they would prove neither uninteresting nor unacceptable, we venture now to exhibit what have been thought by many to demonstrate the superstition of the rabbinical Jew, and the trifling of the Talmud, but which, we honestly confess, we are blind enough not to perceive in any such light. And we think that even the scientific reader, whose religious convictions may be opposed to those of the people to whom these enactments are addressed, will candidly assert that they are by no means of a bad, but of a good, healthy tendency, and are not to be despised. Indeed, many authorities high in the scientific world have already so pronounced, as we may perhaps have occasion to show hereafter. At present we would proceed with the task immediately before us.

In the Mishna which is the text of the Talmud, there is a treatise called חולין *Cholin* i. e. of profane (slaughtering) thus styled in contradistinction to that treatise which discourses of קדשים *Kadashim*, i. e. of sacred (slaughtering) the former, with which we have now to do, treating of the slaughtering of animals required for domestic or secular purposes—the latter, of those devoted to sacrifice. In our extracts from this Mishnic treatise, we shall avail ourselves of the translations and notes of the Rev. Messrs. D. A. De Sola, and Dr. M. J. Raphall, of Dr. Jost, and of the excellent Hebrew commentaries of R. Obadiah Bartenora, and *Tosephet Yom Tob* and also of the *Meloh Caph Nachat* appended to the Berlin edition of the Mishna, (A. M. 5593.)

The first chapter of the treatise *Cholin* treats of the persons qualified, the instruments used, and the mode and place of slaughtering. We shall add a few explanatory words within brackets. §1. All [who are well acquainted with the laws respecting slaughtering] are permitted to slaughter [animals allowed to be eaten,—no priest is required as in the case of sacrifices,] and their slaughtering is *casher.* [To convey what has been properly slaughtered, and may be lawfully eaten, we retain this rabbinical term, or use the English word "proper."] Deaf and dumb or demented persons, or little [young] ones are, however, excepted ; because they are liable to make mistakes in slaughtering, &c.* * * *
[The appointment in Jewish communities of a Shochet, or quali-

---

* The asterisks denote the omission of passages we have considered not immediately connected with our subject.

fied slaughterer is a consequence of the requirements of the Mishna, and where private individuals do not perform the functions of the Shochet, he becomes a salaried officer of the congregation. This is almost universally the case, since the due discharge of his duties requires much time, he having not only to see that the animal or fowl be slain so that the blood flow from it in a proper manner, but having carefully to *examine* the beasts to ascertain that their internal state and conformation be perfectly healthy, ere he can pronounce them fit for food ; but of this more hereafter. The second section of this chapter directs that the slaughtering shall be performed with sharp instruments only, prohibiting those which are at all blunt or jagged, " because these do not cut but strangle," and they therefore not only inflict great and unnecessary pain upon the animal, but prevent *the free flow of blood*, and consequently, as is known, *even affect the state of the flesh.* Testimony to the propriety and value of this enactment of the Mishna, and proof that it, as well as those presently noticed, are good and well calculated to secure *wholesome, healthy meat*, more especially with reference to the flowing of the blood from the animal we find supplied not only by Dr. Townley, as quoted above, but by that high authority, the celebrated Dr. Andrew Duncan, late Professor of Medical Jurisprudence in the University of Edinburgh. He says, " *The mode of killing has considerable effect on the flesh of the animal.* * * The common mode of killing animals in this kingdom is by striking them on the forehead with a pole-axe, and then cutting their throats to bleed them. But this method is cruel and not free from danger. The animal is not always brought down by the first blow, and the repetition is difficult and uncertain , and if the animal be not very well secured, accidents may happen. Lord Somerville* therefore endeavoured to introduce the method of pithing or laying cattle by dividing the spinal marrow above the origin of the phrenic nerves, as is commonly practised in Barbary and Spain, Portugal, Jamaica, and in some parts of England ; and Mr. Jackson says that " the best method of killing a bullock is by the thrusting a sharp pointed knife into the spinal marrow when the bullock will immediately fall without a struggle ; then cut the arteries above the heart.† Although the operation of pithing is not so difficult, but that it may after some practice be performed with tolerable certainty, and although Lord Somerville took a man with him to Portugal to be instructed in the method, and made it a condition that the prize cattle should be pithed instead

---

* General Survey of the Agriculture of Shropshire. By Joseph Plymley, M. A. 8vo., London, 1803, p. 243.

† Reflections on the Commerce of the Mediterranean. By John Jackson, Esq., F. S. A., 8vo., London, 1804, p. 91.

of being knocked down, still *pithing is not becoming general in England.* This may be partly owing to prejudice; but we have been told that the flesh of the cattle killed in this way in Portugal is *very dark*, and *becomes soon putrid*, probably from the animal *not bleeding* well, in consequence of the action of the heart being interrupted before the vessels of the neck are divided. It therefore becomes *preferable to bleed the animal to death directly, as is practised by the Jewish butchers.* The Mosaic law so strictly prohibits the eating of blood that the Talmud contains a body of regulations concerning the killing of animals; and the Jews as a point of religion will not eat the flesh of any animal not killed by a butcher of their own persuasion. Their method is to tie all the four feet of the animal together, bring it to the ground, and turning its head back, to cut the throat at once down to the bone with a long, very sharp, but not pointed knife, dividing all the large vessels of the neck. In this way the blood is discharged quickly and completely. The effect is indeed said to be so very obvious, that some Christians will eat no meat but what has been killed by a Jew butcher." Dr. Duncan further remarks, " Domestic birds in general are killed in a very unskilful and barbarous manner," and after detailing those methods, his further remarks tend to show that those laid down and required by the Mishna is the most merciful, and in every way the best. But for these details we must refer the reader to the learned writer himself.* We have made the above lengthy extract from him because it conveys our own convictions, and in language preferable to our own, since it furnishes the unbiassed testimony to the wisdom and principles of the directions for slaughtering given by the Mishna of one highly esteemed in the scientific world; one, also, who, if he have a religious leaning at all in what he writes, cannot certainly be suspected of its being towards the ritual of the Jews. Founded upon the same reasons, and having the same object are the following five traditional rules which are to be strictly observed in killing cattle or fowl, or they become *Pasool*, *i. e.*, unlawful to be used for food. In slaughtering there must not be 1st, שהייה *i. e. delay*—as when a person cuts a little of the throat of the animal, then stops, and cuts again, and continues in the same manner till the act of killing is completed. 2nd. דרסה *i. e. pressure*,—when the cutting was effected by pressure only, without passing the knife to and fro on the animals throat; or cutting off the head or tubes by a single stroke, using the knife like a hatchet or sword. 3rd. חלדה *i. e. concealment*, —when the knife was covered with any thing; for instance, if it was covered or hidden by the wool of the animal, or by a cloth, or that it

---

* See Encyclopædia Brittanica Art. Food.

was passed between the tubes, and the killing completed by cutting the tubes either upwards or downwards. 4th. הנגרמה *i. e. deviation,*—when the cutting has been beyond the bounds or limits on the throat of the animal, and it was made either above or below these limits indicated by the Mishna. 5th. עיקור *i. e. tearing,*—when the tubes of any of them had been forcibly torn away before the act of killing was completed. (For more detailed particulars the Hebrew reader is referred to the Talmud, Treatise *Cholin* p. 9., and Maimonides chap. iii. of *Hilchoth Shechitah,* in vol. ii. of *Yad Hachazakah.* Grounded upon these reason also are the immediately following directions in §3 and in the following Mishnic sections.] §4. An animal which was slaughtered by being cut at either side of the throat is Cashér. * * If an animal was cut from the neck downwards, [that is, if the incision was made on the top of the neck, through the vertebra before the knife reached the œsophagus and trachea,] it becomes unlawful for use. * * An animal which is cut below the throat is Cashér. * * Chapter ii., § 1. When one of the pipes [*i. e.* the trachea] has been cut through in killing fowl, and both [the trachea and œsophagus] in killing cattle they are Cashér, [but are only so when it has thus happened unpremeditatedly, for it is necessary to commence the act of slaughtering with the intention of cutting through both tubes. For the purpose of securing a perfect flow of blood, the following remark of R. Yehudah is directed.] It is necessary that in killing fowl the veins at the sides of the throat should also be cut through. [With the same intent, come the concluding requirements of this section.] If but one half [of the trachea] is cut through in fowl, and one and a-half [*i. e.* the trachea, and half of the œsophagus] in cattle, it is unfit; but if the greater part of one tube is cut through in fowl and the greater part of the two in cattle, it is Cashér."

Here we conclude, for the present, our quotations from the treatise " Cholin," having exhibited in them the principal directions and requirements of the Mishna, concerning that part of slaughtering which has reference to the extraction of the animals blood, and which as we have before seen, has so much to do with the healthiness of the meat. We shall have occasion again to refer to this treatise when examining other matters connected with our main subject. And now in accordance with the plan laid down, * we will endeavor to supply a synopsis of those further rabbinical regulations and directions for the avoidance of blood-eating, and state the penalties resulting from infringement or neglect of this sanatory law. The Yad Hachazakah of Maimonides contains such a synopsis,† and we will now endeavor briefly to scan it.

*Vide page 26.
†Vide vol. 2, Book 5, ch. 6. *Treatise on Forbidden Food.*

Maimonides writes, § 1—He who wilfully eats of blood of [the quantity of] an olive, incurs the penalty of excision, [Lev. vii. 26-27] but if through error, he becomes liable to the bringing of an appointed sin offering. The law explains that he becomes not liable but for all blood of beasts [wild and domestic] and of fowl, whether clean or unclean, as it is said, "And ALL blood shall you NOT eat in all your habitations, whether of fowl or of beast (behemah). Wild animals are included here in the term 'behemah,' for we find it elsewhere said [Deut. xiv. 4-5] These are the beasts (habehemah) which ye may eat, the ox, &c., the hart and the roebuck &c., but to the blood of fish, locusts, insects and the like, the above law applies not; wherefore the blood of fish locusts, &c., which are clean is permitted. * * * But of those which are unclean it is forbidden, because it forms the main substance of their body ; and it is with their flesh as with the fat of the unclean beast. § 2. Human blood is prohibited from the authority of the Scribes ; an infringement of this prohibition subjects the offender to the flogging of rebellion*. § 3. The penalty of excision applies only to that blood which issues at the time of slaughtering, or drawn while it yet retains its red particles ; to that blood which has entered the heart, and to that which results from phlebotomy, and yet issues forth ; but that which issues at the beginning of the bleeding, and that which appears when the flow begins to cease, these do not cause the penalty of excision, but are in this respect like the blood of members, since that which flowed through the bleeding, was the vital blood. § 4. The substantial blood and blood of the members, such as of the spleen, kidneys, &c., of eggs, and that found in the heart at the time of slaughtering, as also blood found in the liver, does not create the penalty of excision, and he who eats thereof, even a quantity equal to an olive, incurs according to the divine law the penalty of castigation,

*As emphatically exhibiting the extreme care and scrupulousness to be employed by Jews in refraining from blood-eating, we might have quoted above, the following words of Maimonides in the same paragraph,—"but to eat the blood from the teeth (gums,) is of course not preventible ; thus, if he bites into a piece of bread and observes there blood (from the gums) he cuts away that part and afterwards eats." Thus writes Maimonides. Another celebrated Jewish Doctor Menasseh Ben Israel, whilst engaged in the days of Cromwell to secure the return of his people to England, in adverting to the ignorant and fanatic prejudice which had been raised against them for " using human blood to make their Passover cakes," says, (Vindiciæ Judæorum sec.1. See Samuels, "Jerusalem," by Mendelsohn, vol. 1. p. 5.) " And more than this, if they find one drop of blood in an egg, they (the Jews) cast it away as prohibited; and if in eating a piece of bread, it happens to touch any blood drawn from the teeth or gums, it must be pared and cleansed from the said blood, as it evidently appears from *Shulchan Aruch* and our ritual book, &c.

for it is said 'ye shall eat *no* blood.' And with reference to the penalty of excision, the text saith, 'for the life of the flesh is in the blood,' implying that excision is only incurred by eating of that blood with which the life went forth. The blood of a fœtus found in the uterus of any animal is to be accounted as the blood of one born, therefore the blood found in its heart causes the penalty of excision, but the rest of its blood is to be accounted as the blood of members. In § 6 particular directions are laid down for extracting the blood from the heart, which, being so to speak, the blood-pump of the wondrous mansion in which it resides, requires such particular directions. In § 7 are given directions for extracting the blood from the liver, so that it may escape freely and not be retained by anything. In § 9 we find that if the neck of a beast become broken, before it dies the blood becomes unduly absorbed in the members, and then it is prohibited ; if, however, in killing (healthy) animals or fowl, no blood issues, they are lawful for food. The following directions are worthy of note, as being now actually observed by the great body of Jews in every part of the world, even by that comparatively small portion of them who do not generally guide themselves by rabbinical teachings, but who yet observe these we are about to mention, as good, proper, and wholesome practices. How far they are calculated to procure to these observers good, wholesome meat, may be decided by reference to Doctor Duncan above quoted, and to other writers. § 10. Meat cannot be considered as free from blood unless it have been duly salted and expressed after the following manner. The blood must first be drawn from the meat, which is then to be carefully salted, and is to remain in salt for a time (not less) than that consumed in walking a mile, [half an hour to an hour is the time observed by Jewish families] afterwards it is to be drained until the water which runs from it is clear, when it is to be placed in water before using. § 11. The salting process should only be carried on in a perforated vessel [cullender,] so that the blood escape, and then with coarse salt, since fine becomes imbibed in the flesh, but does not extract the blood."

Were it consistent with our limits, and necessary to our subject, we might by further quotations shew even more clearly the scrupulousness of the Hebrews in abstaining from blood. We might describe the diligence and care employed by them in purging from their meat, before eating, all veins and arteries, without which process, the meat would be considered as improper for food, and as so much carrion. But we think it enough to inform the reader of these facts, and to refer him to the books already mentioned for further details. For now we would bring our remarks on the prohibition of blood to a close. These few considerations however, we would urge in conclusion—The Hebrew people for thousands of years, even before those glorious days when their great MOSES lived and moved among them have been in a most remarkably scrupulous manner observant of this prohibition. They have regarded the eating of blood as an abomination, and as a loathsome practice; as a practice, which, if much indulged in, would cause them to think lightly even of the blood of their fellow-men. And what, to them, have been the results of this, *nationally*, and *after so very long a space of time*?—for it is only by referring to them as a nation, and to the longest period to which we can look back, that the question ought to refer, and that we ought to judge it. In the remarks we have made upon this sanatory law, as it undoubtedly is, of the Hebrews, we have deemed it proper briefly to show that scientific writers of the highest reputation have proved, that the wholesomeness of animal food has much to do with the extraction or non-extraction of the vital stream, and that, as a consequence, our own health is, in no inconsiderable degree, dependant thereupon. Let us now ask, whether their abstinence from blood through ages has at all made the Hebrews physically speaking, a less healthy or favored people than those who do not so abstain, and whether they do not rather present the most powerful and conclusive testimony in support of those writers who contend for the utility and importance of the prohibition—writers whose humble disciple, apart from our peculiar religious convictions, we profess to be. These queries we make without stopping to insist upon their comparative exemption from that class of diseases from which, they ought, as a consequence of their abstinence, to be free, but to which those who unreservedly indulge in such gross indigestible nutriment should be subject; nor do we stop to insist upon the probability of their being less likely to become legitimate objects for the attacks of epidemics, &c., than those who are less careful than they in this regard, and in the general healthiness of their animal food; but we go on to remark, that although our limits as well as our inclination, have caused us to confine the number of our references and authorities, still, we think we have adduced sufficient respectable testimony to show, that blood-eating exercises a decidedly "baneful influence on the disposition" and *minds* of men. Christian writers have uniformly endeavored to show—with what success we need not here inquire, that the rabbinical traditions are but little older than Christianity. Supposing this to be the case, and confining our retrospective view of the mental condition of the Hebrew people to nineteen centuries, let us ask, and let the reader decide in all candor, whether that, by all acknowledged, wondrous activity and

elasticity of intellect which has ever characterised them; which has
enabled them, under God, to bear up against persecution the most in-
tense; and slaughter the most bloody ; to withstand like an impreg-
nable fortress, those destructive causes and events which have swept
away nations more numerous, more powerful, and in every way more
prosperous than they—have swept them away so that scarcely a ves-
tige remains of them;—let us ask, whether this, and their equally acknowledged exemption from the commission of those fearful deeds of
violence and bloodshed, which are but too frequently the result of an
artificially-formed brutish organisation and instincts; of a superinduced
animalism, which is but too surely the offspring of unrestrained indulgence in matters dietetic; whether these facts prove that the prohibition of blood and other articles of diet has acted injuriously to
them, or whether they do not present testimony valuable and conclusive for those advocates of total abstinence from blood-eating who
show that the mind, equally with the body, must at last suffer from
the practice.   We humbly claim for these questions the same indulgent
and serious consideration* which thinking and good men who are well-
wishers of their fellows have very properly extended to that great moral
movement—the total abstinence from intoxicating drinks.   The percep-
tive faculties may become clouded, men may " become drunken with
blood-drinking" also, saith the prophet ; and were the ill effects of the
latter so immediately perceivable, and its opponents as numerous, and as
zealous, as are the advocates of the former movement, then would there

* We have seen with as much surprise as regret, that an able writer should des-
cend to treat lightly a question which has had for its supporters so many master
minds--advocates as pious and amiable as they were learned; of course we can
have but little to say to remarks conceived in such a spirit, but this much we would
observe.   To select the Canadian *habitants* with whose unrestrained addiction to
blood-eating we are sufficiently acquainted, as a proof of the non-injuriousness of the
practice, we deem singularly unfortunate, though not for our assertion above made
with reference to its effects, mentally.   We only speak, as we can only speak, be it
remembered, of the testimony afforded by nations after the lapse of a long period of
time, say of centuries, and thus it will be perceived that we only speak of blood-
eating as being an element—how powerful, who shall say when it is so announced
and condemned by inspiration—of decay and destruction in a nation.   With individual cases the question has nothing to do—we will not, nor did we ever maintain
that with reference to these, the practice is a bad one; but to return.   The Canadian
habitants are doubtless, a worthy, happy, contented, and so far as creature com-
forts, and, perhaps, business transactions, are concerned, an acute people, yet
few would charge them with too much intellectuality, enterprise, or with a too
free spirit of inquiry either in matters spiritual or secular.   Of course with other
nations there may be, and indeed are, other causes and agencies, educational especially, to counteract this serious error in diet ; just as it has been shown other dietetic
substances may counteract the ill effects of eating blood, in the individual system.

doubtlessly exist in many men's minds the same antipathy against the one usage, as for the abuse of the other. But be this as it may, this much appears evident and sure to us with reference to the ideas and sentiments of the people whom the question at present most concerns. We believe it unquestionable that irrespective of the in-uperable religious objections they have to blood eating, the conviction is deeply rooted and generally felt among all Israelites, that would they not snap asunder one of the most powerful links in their national union and preservation, but would they maintain the undying vigor of their race—would they exempt their bodies from gross scorbutic humors and affections, and their minds from those passions and tendencies which weaken what is strong, depress what is exalted, degrade what is elevated, and brutalise what is divine,—then they must not lightly esteem, but strictly and religiously observe and respect THE PROHIBITION OF BLOOD.

CHAPTER III.

OF BEASTS CLEAN AND UNCLEAN.

WHAT has just been remarked as to the convictions and usages of the Hebrew people with reference to the Prohibition of Blood, mainly applies to their abstinence from the flesh of such animals as are pronounced by the Scriptures and their ritual code to be טמא (tameh) unclean, אסור (assur) prohibited, or טרפה (terefa) torn. As will be presently seen, their traditions and authoritative writings ascribe moral, as well as hygienic, reasons for the Mosaic distinction of animals, and for the institution of those directions and enactments which lead them to reject as impure and unhealthy, such species of animal food as are commonly and unhesitatingly received by other nations, as ordinary and acceptable articles of diet. We have already made slight allusion to the fact, that as early as the days of Noah, a distinction of " clean beasts" and " beasts which are not clean"* was made and known. But

---

* " A remarkable instance of circumlocution," says Raphall, "cited as a proof of the extreme purity of mind of the sacred author, who uses these three words to avoid saying טמאה (temeah) which in the Hebrew, does not simply express *the negation of clean*, as do the corresponding negatives in other language, viz: the Greek *akathartos*, the Latin *impurus*, the French *immonde*, the Spanish *immundo*, the Italian *immondo*, the German *unrein*, the Sweedish *oreen*, the Danish *orehn*, the English *unclean*, the Polish *eniczyotc*, &c., but has a positive meaning, the counter-sense of טהורה (tehorah) *clean*, and the extreme counter-sense of קדוש (kadosh) *holy*; and denotes a moral as well as physical state, which in any other language, we want an analogous single word to express."

D

we shall not stop now to discuss at all that very debatable question,
whether the distinction of animals here referred to, is identical with that
made in Leviticus,* and if so, being known and observed, equally
with the prohibition to eat blood, by the Noachidœ,—whether these two
laws can now lay claim to other than Jewish attention and observance;
—whether the terms " clean"and " unclean" refer simply and respectively to those animals which were used or rejected for sacrifices, or
whether, as Jahn seems to think† the distinction only conveys that
before the deluge, the flesh of animals was converted into food ;—these
being perhaps purely theological questions, which, however interesting,
we may not stop here, to entertain.‡ We merely remind our readers that
in addition to this distinction, a further one is made (ch. viii, v. 20,) with
reference to fowls, and will proceed with them to the eleventh chapter
of Leviticus where we find not only general rules of discrimination laid
down, but also a catalogue given of various oviparous and viviparous
creatures, forbidden to Israel throughout their generations.   This chapter we propose to examine at length, availing ourself of such expositions
and illustrations as, in the first place, the Hebrews themselves afford us ;
and secondly, of such as are supplied us by Christian commentators.
And in this course, our attention will be necessarily directed among
others to the following important points:—

First, The general directions for discrimination supplied ;

Secondly, The nomenclature of the animals and their nature; and

Thirdly, Their prohibition ; having reference to authority and reason.

The chapter commences with the law of discrimination respecting

---

* We learn that Noah " took of every clean beast and of every clean
fowl, and offered burnt offerings on the altar." This circumstance has much to do
with the origin of the opinion respecting the use and meaning of the term " clean,"
as applied thus early to animals, though it would seem to furnish a powerful argument against the assumption that it refers to such animals only as were used for
sacrifices ; since from this passage we are almost obliged to conclude that the distinction was known to Noah, before he made his sacrifice, for which he *selected.*
Philipson (Apud De Sola and Raphall's Translation of the Scriptures) seems
to incline to this opinion, when he says : " It is natural to make a distinction between
animals proper to be offered as a sacrifice to the Deity, and such as are improper
for that purpose, including all that are carnivorous. This distinction we find esta-
bli shed among all ancient nations."

† See his " Biblical Archœology" § 136, p. 147, Ed. Andover, 1827.

‡ Perhaps Rashi's gloss on Gen. vii, 2, may be considered as enunciatory of
Jewish tradition and opinion on this question. On the words " of all clean beasts,"
he says, העתידה להיות טהורה לישראל למדנו שלמד נח תורה " That is, which are
hereafter to be considered clean by all Israel. Hence we learn, that the Eternal taught
the law to Noah." i. e. anticipated to him a subsequent revelation to Moses.

beasts. (Verse 1) " The Eternal spake unto Moses and unto Aaron, saying unto them, V. 2. Speak unto the children of Israel saying, 'These are the beasts * which ye may eat from [among] all the beasts that are on the earth. V. 3. Whatever parteth the hoof and is cloven footed *and* cheweth the cud among the beasts, that may ye eat. V. 4. Nevertheless these may ye not eat, of them that chew the cud or of them that divide the hoof ; the camel, &c." Here follows an enumeration of various beasts to be noticed hereafter ; we proceed to the 9th verse which contains the distinctive signs of permitted fishes. " These may ye eat of all that are in the waters ; whatsoever hath fins and scales in the waters, in the sea and in the rivers, them may ye eat. V. 10. And all that have not fins nor scales in the seas and in the rivers, of all that move in the waters, and of any living thing which is in the waters; they shall be an abomination unto you." This much of the distinctive signs of permitted and prohibited fishes. For birds there are no distinctive signs given; but we are told, V. 20, " all fowls that creep going upon *all* four, shall be an abomination unto you. Yet, these may ye eat, of every flying, creeping thing that goeth upon *all* four which have legs above their feet to leap withal upon the earth ; even these of them ye may eat, the locust, &c., V. 23. But all other flying, creeping things, which have four feet *shall be* an abomination unto you." In verse 27, we find further that, " whosoever goeth upon his paws among all manner of beasts that go on *all* four, those are unclean unto you, &c." Such are the general rules for discrimination, supplied us by the Scriptures. And before giving a closer attention to them, it becomes us to admit with Fleury, that it was not peculiar to the Hebrews, to abstain from certain animals out of a religious principle, for the neighbouring people did the same. Neither the Syrians nor the Egyptians eat any fish ; and some have thought it was superstition, that made the ancient Greeks not eat it. The Egyptians of Thebes, would eat no mutton, because they worshipped Ammon under the shape of a ram,† but they killed goats. In other places, they abstained from goats flesh, and sacrificed sheep. The Egyptian priests used no meat nor drink imported from foreign countries,‡ and as to the product of their own, besides fish, they abstained from beasts that have a round foot, or divided into several toes, or that have no horns, and birds that live upon flesh. Many would eat nothing that had life ; and in the times of their purification, they would not touch so much as eggs, herbs, or garden stuff. None of the Egyptians would eat

* From the wording of this text, which is strictly in the present tense, singular number, and means literally, " This is the living creature" or beast, Rashi says that Moses exhibited to the people all the various creatures he mentions.

† Herod. ii.   ‡ Porphyr. Abstin. iv.

beans.* They accounted swine unclean ; whoever touched one, though in passing by, washed himself and his clothes. Socrates, in his commonwealth, reckons eating swine's flesh among the superfluous things introduced by luxury.† Every one knows that the Indian Brahmins, still, neither eat nor kill any sort of animal ; and it is certain they have not done it for more than two thousand years.

But if there be nothing peculiar in the Israelites, at the command of Moses, abstaining from the flesh of certain animals from religious motives there is yet that which we shall find original, wise and salutary in this Mosaic prohibition. We ought not to commence any such investigation, however, until, in accordance with the advice which the learned Mendelssohn gives, we first fix the correct sense of some of the most important terms connected with our present subject, and which to avoid misconception and confusion, we shall endeavor to ascertain ; yet, as some may regard such inquiries, which will be almost exclusively philological, as neither necessary nor interesting ; we will present them in the form of notes, to be read or to be passed over at pleasure, for that which they may regard as having more to do with the main subject.*

---

* Herod. ii.

† Plato ii Rep.

‡ חיה *Chaya* and בהמה *Behemah*, In verse 2 of the 11th chapter of Leviticus, the Anglican translation renders *Zot hachayah* by "These are the beasts," *Behemah*, in the same verse, is also translated, "beasts." The Spanish Jewish translators, Menasseh Ben Israel, Serrano, Fernandes and Diaz, translate *hachayah*, we think with better taste, by *animales* and *behemah* by *quadropea*. De Reyna, however, generally so correct, here renders both by *animales*. Mendelssohn's German Jewish translation has respectively *thiere* and *thiern*, which, according to Weber, may mean either *animal, beast*, or *quadruped ;* and so has the German Christian translators. But the Targum of Onkelos has for the first חיתא ; (chayta) for the second בעירא (bengira.) All leixicographers of note agree in deriving it from the root חיה (chayoh) to live. Among them, R. David Kimchi (Shorashim). So also Furst, who says it means *quidquid vivit, animal, de feris potissimum ;* so too, Gesenius, who explains it as implying the beasts of the field, often opposed to tame animals (behemah) Gen. 1.24, but sometimes including them, Lev. 11. 2. So Newman. Leigh, in his learned "Critica Sacra" and his French translator DeWolzogue, are of the same opinion. But Parkhurst, perhaps more correctly, thinks the primary meaning of the root to denote *vigor,* power ; he says as the noun it includes birds, beasts and reptiles, Gen. viii. 17, exclusive of fish and fowl, Gen. 1. 28, but frequently a wild beast as being more vigorous and lively than the tame species, Gen. i. 25. The Aruch from the Gemara of Cholin shows us (as did Maimonides in the extract elsewhere taken from him) that *chayah* is sometimes included in the term *behemah* and vice versa, *behemah* in the term *chayah.* And Rashi, in his comment on this verse, calls our attention to the same fact. In the Hebrew commentary to that edition of the Pentateuch, known as Mendlessohn's* we find the following remarks by that able gram-

*Ed. Berlin, 1832.

The result of such a critical examination of the text would be to establish, first, as regards *beasts*, that all which possess hoofs that are cloven or bifurcated, that is, which are clearly and unmistakably divided into two parts or hoofs, and which also and at the same time, chew the cud, or ruminate, are to be accounted as clean and proper for food;

marion Herts Wessely. "The word *chaya* includes all species (genera) man, beast, fowl and reptile; since all these possess a living being (nefesh chaya). In proof of this we find Gen. i. 'Let the earth bring forth every living creature (nefesh chaya) after its kind, beasts, reptiles and the beasts of the earth, after its kind.' The first (*nefesh chaya*) is the general expression; 'beasts, reptiles, and beasts of the earth' is the particularisation thereof. The meaning of the text here, then, is 'This is the living creature which you may eat of all creatures having a living being or 'existence.' In the derivation of *behemah*, the Hebrew grammarians concur, also referring it to the Arabic, or rather Ethiopic *bahm*, which means to be silent, dumb. It occurs not as a verb in Hebrew. As a noun Furst says it means " *bestia domestica quae opponitur feræ* chaya *jumenta, greges et omne omnino domesticum pecus.*" According to David Levy, Gesenius and Newman, it denotes *tame cattle* if in opposition to *chaya*; and *large cattle* when in opposition to *mikneh*, (small cattle); Parkhurst gives its meanings 1.—Any brute, opposed to man. 2.—Any terrestrial quadruped, viviparous and of some size. 3.—A tame animal. Raphall says " In the Hebrew, "behemah" is used for *domestic animal*, and " chayah" *wild animal*. Some, however, are of opinion that all herbivorous animals, whether domestic or wild, are called "behemah," and that all carnivorous animals are designated by "chayah," Mendelssohn. We give the comment in Mendlessohn's Pentateuch (by Herts Wessely) on the word occurring Lev. xi., " All living creatures are included in the term *nefesh chaya*, even man, since it is said man became a *nefesh chaya* or living being. Wherefore, in speaking of the wild beasts of the forest, &c., an adjective, predicate or attribute is to be used. Thus we say, *chaya rangah* evil or ferocious beast, as Jacob in Gen. 37, so *chayat hasadeh* field-beast, Lev. xxvi.; so too *chayat haarets*, beasts of the earth Gen. i.; *chayat yangar* forest-beasts, Isa. 26. The term is especially applied to ferocious predatory creatures because of their extreme strength and vigor, while domestic animals are termed " behemah." Be it known also that " behemah" (is a common noun, and) includes all the species of animals walking earth, man excepted; as we find in Psalm xxxvi., " Man and beasts (behemah) wilt thou save, O, Lord," where it includes wild and domestic creatures; so also in 1 Samuel, ch. xvii. " the fowl of heaven, and beasts (behemah) of the field, &c., &c." The above shows us, as would also some slight acquaintance with Hebrew writers, that *chaya* means generally, though not always, *wild* beasts, and *behemah*, *domestic* animals.

מפרסת *Maphreset* and פרסה *Parsah* correctly rendered in the Anglican version, " divideth the hoof." All grammarians refer the root of these two words to פרס (Paros) or with a ש (seen) שרפ, meaning *to break* or *to divide*. Thus we have Furst and Buxtorf, giving the significations of the verb. 1. *frangere*. 2. *dividere*: and of the noun, *pars findens, acuta ad scindendum et effodiendum* (syn. אגך ungula) *uncus, unguis, ungula* (Klaue Huf) *non de fissa solum quæ* מפרסת פרסה *nominatur sed utraque utpote ad inuncandum destinata, &c.*" " As a noun, the hoof of such animals whether divided before, as the ox, sheep, goat, hog, Deut. xiv. 4-8, or divided only behind as the horse,"—Parkhurst. Men, ben Israel and Fernandes

and as such, may be used by the Hebrews. This will be further seen by the examination following of some of their most eminent and authoritative writers. We commence by translating from the commentary of the learned and elegant Abarbanel on the 11th chapter of Leviticus.

translate *unan una*; De Reyna—*animal de pezuno*; Serrano—*qui tiene pezuno*. The German translators,—*Klauen Spaltet*. Herts Wessely makes on these words the following remarks : "Rashi maintains that the meaning of *Maphreset* is as given in the Targum of Onkelos, viz: סדיקה (sedica) *dividing*, that *Parsah* is synonimous with *Plante* (in French) and that *Shossangat Shessang* means the hoof being divided above and beneath into two claws or nails—as the Targum has it, ומטלפא טילפין *oomtalpha teelpeen*, [cloven footed] for that there are some animals having their hoofs divided above, but not completely divided, being joined beneath." According to this explanation of Rashi, *Maphreset and Parsah* have not the same meaning ; since *Maphreset* implies *division*, as in Danl. v., and *Parsah* means *the sole of the foot*. If it be affirmed, that according to the opinion of our Rabbi, that every hand or foot having divided fingers or claws be called *Parsa*, then should the human hand also be so called. Rashbam, however, explains the terms as implying one perfect hoof, like a shoe, and not as conveying nails or claws upon each finger like the *shafan* and *arnebet* have, and *Shossanget Shessang* implies the division of the hoof into two, and its not being one, as in the case of the horse and ass. According to this explanation, which I adopt, the text teaches what here follows :— ' Every beast which, from its birth, divideth the hoof, having on its foot a shoe-like hoof covering the foot, and is further divided in such a manner as to present the appearance of two hoofs, may be regarded as clean for food ; and I am of opinion that the foot having a shoe-like hoof, is what is called in the sacred tongue *Parsa*, because it (the hoof) covers the foot, and is synonimous with *oopharesu* in the passage *oopharesu hasimlah* (they shall spread the garment), Deut. xx 2. Num. iv. &c. So when the word *Parus* occurs either with *sheen* or *samech* it means to spread, since these letters [being included by Hebrew grammarians in one class] frequently interchange with each other. But Radak in his *Shorashim* Radix *Paras* says, that even if written with a *seen* the word *Paros* has always for its radical meaning *to cut*, and it is thus used metaphorically to express pangs of the body through sorrow, (Jer. xiv, Sam. 1.) This, however, is not my opinion ; but I believe they all convey the idea of spreading. See 2nd Chr. vi. Ex. 37 ; and with reference to all the passages cited by Kimchi, I remark that in cases of deep grief, it occurs that the sufferers *spread forth* their hands; so the cloth is *spread* on the table for food in the case of the mourner. *Perusa* and *Paros*, (with Samech) is Chaldaic, as in Daniel (loc. cit.) According to my explanation, then, it is not proper to apply the term *Parsah* to the sole of the foot, generally, but to those animals only which have a shoe-like hoof covering the foot, as in the case of the ox, ass, horse, &c. But the sole of the foot of other animals which have toes or claws, and upon every toe a nail, is not called Parsa in the scriptures on any one occasion. See Isa. v. 28, Jer. xlvii. Ex. xxii &c." The learned Mendelssohn in a note to this comment of Wessely adopts his ideas, and changes his German translation in accordance therewith. We are bold enough, however, to dissent from such high authorities, and after deliberation are yet of opinion that the *primary* idea of the word Paros is to divide, as it has been given by almost all lexicographers, and by the ancient He-

He writes—"Every animal having hoofs, and this hoof split or divided into two, possesses the first requisite of the text; the second requisite is, that the animal chew the cud, or ruminate. Possessing these two conditions, it is clean, and permitted to be eaten. It is not, however, the intention of the text to imply that these requisites render the animal, clean *per se*, or their absence, unclean *per se*; but it

brew Commentators. R. Wessely's idea of "*spreading* the cloth" in the passage referred to, we cannot but think exceedingly fanciful, and not warranted by a knowledge of Eastern customs; besides *spreading*, especially in the case particularly mentioned, is only *dividing* the folds, and placing flat, the garment preserved in a folded form by the wifes parents. So the hands being held out in grief is merely an elaboration of the primary meaning of the root, since they then become *divided* from the body, as compared to their position, or separated, when in a state of rest. But we must not continue longer this inquiry. We will only say that Serrano in his Spanish Jewish version, (A. M. 5455) which it is probable Wessely follows, already translates in accordance with such an opinion, since he has—"qui tiene pesuno *y este pesuno hendido* en differentes"

שסעת *Shossangat* and שסע *Shessang.* These words are by all referred to the root *Shassong* which means to cleave or divide. "*Incidere, discindere velut de ungulis animalium divisis quæ a pedis parte posteriore connexæ sunt*—Furst. *Findere. Diffind. Discind. Bifidum, Bifidatum esse.*"—Buxt. " This word is applied to those animals that are cloven footed, i e. whose hoofs are not only divided into two parts or claws, but those two claws cleft from each other without any connecting membrane—Park. It is rendered by the Spanish Jewish translators—*y hendien hendedura de unas,* or, *qui tiene los pesunos hedidos.*

מעלת *Mangalat* and נרה *Gerah.* The root of the first word all agree to be *ngaloh,* to ascend; in Hiphil, *ascendere faciens*; *Gerah* is also generally admitted to mean the cud, *rumen,* the contents of the stomach which the animal chews again. In opposition to many, Furst derives it from נרר *Gerar,* "significatio—*ruminatio pabulum ruminatum* in phrasi, *Gerah Gerar de cibi retractione atque reciprocatione.*" So also Gesenius who makes יגר (Lev. xi. 7) to be the future tense *Niphal.* It means strictly, says Parkhurst, to stir or raise up the cud from the rumen or first stomach, Deut. xiv. 8. *Veloh Gerah.,* according to either translation the ה (he) in *gerah* agreeing with *chazeer,* masc must here be radical—Parkhurst. The following, cited by the *Moosaph Hearuch,* furnishes additional Talmudic exposition, The references are to Mish. ch. 2 of *Yomah,* and ch. 3 of *Tamid.* ממקום שחותך הראש
עד הצלעות נקרא נרה והוא כנגד החזה והוא אבר אחד שמוליך אדם אחד. Wessely in his comment, after explaining the term to be chewing the cud, calls attention to the remark of Kimchi, who says the root of *Gerah* is probably identical with the noun, but refers it to the *Kephulim,* or verbs having a duplicate radical, from its affinity to *Garon* and *Gargeret.* After quoting Rashi's Gloss on these words, he approves the opinion which refers it to the root Gerar, the *Gimmel* receiving *Tsere* to compensate for the omission of *Dagesh* in the *Resh,* Then, after dissenting from Rashi's views respecting the word *Gerirah,* he adds, *Mangaleh Gerah* means the reascension of the rumen and its remastication and deglutition, according to the translation of Onkelos who renders it by מסקא פשרא [Maska Phishrah] *Pishra* being the Chaldaic for cud, as *Gerah* is the term applied to the ascending rumen in animals which are clean."

teaches us, that these are the signs by which we are to pronounce the animal clean for man's food, or the reverse; that is, that the flesh of the animals possessing these requisites, is, for the most part, proper and good for man's diet. Thus, the reason why animals chew the cud, is, that they have no grinders [incisors] in the upper jaw, wherewith duly to grind or masticate their food; and on which account they are unable to eat any hard substance but vegetable matter which they swallow whole, and which, when softened in the stomach through the natural heat, &c., is regurgitated into the throat again, for further mastication and deglutition. Animals of this order are mostly obese and best adapted to become food for man, since they can find their food at all times and in all places; their fat also, is, comparatively speaking, better distributed than with other classes of animals, because they feed upon vegatation, both green and dry, which does not yield gross nutriment;—such animals are not ferocious nor predaceous. In addition to this, they possess a broad and divided hoof; wherefore they do not require claws like those beasts which prey upon human beings or other animals; which kind of food produces in these latter, a hot dry temperament and cruel disposition: * but the former ' walk the earth' eating the produce of the field. In this connexion we have to remark that the prophet Isaiah (upon whom be peace) shows us that at the time of the future redemption, " *the lion shall eat straw like the ox*," on which account " they shall not hurt nor destroy," and that " the wolf shall dwell with the lamb, and the leopard shall lie down with the kid, *and the cow and the bear shall feed together*," because the preying on flesh and blood is [both] the cause [and effect] of their objectionable temperament, and of their trampling upon and seizing what they require. Nature, on this account, has prepared for them claws and fitting grinders to tear their food; but for the clean animals, whose food is the grass of the field, she has prepared divided and broad hoofs, as their manner of walking on the earth to gather their food therefrom requires; nor has she bestowed on them grinders or incisors since these are not required for vegetable food." Abarbanel next proceeds to remark on some of the beasts mentioned in the sacred text, which will be hereafter noticed. We will continue some further observations of this celebrated Jewish commentator, having a closer connexion with those just quoted: thinking that our readers will not be uninterested to see, for the first time in an English dress, the continuation of what we may regard as a brief Hebrew treatise on Zoology,

---

* Compare this remark of Abarbanel with what has been advanced by modern scientific writers as to the effects of blood-eating. See also p 26.

which, although republished by Don Isaac Abarbanel some three
centuries and a half past only, was actually taught in the schools of the
Hebrews some fifteen centuries back ; for our author advances nothing
that is not to be found in the Talmud, and as we have elsewhere said,
the Talmud is a mere compilation of ancient teachings in Israel. But
prior to continuing the Rabbi's remarks, let us make a few of our own
on what has been already advanced from him. The reader will, doubtless, readily perceive their pertinency to the main question, since they
involve inquiries elucidatory of the nature of the clean and unclean
animals.

We observe, in the first place, a remarkable identity in the
definitions of the ruminating animals as given by Abarbanel and the
Talmud, and by modern naturalists. Let us compare his definitions
with those of the illustrious and world-renowned Cuvier. In his
Règne Animal, he gives the following definition of the *Ruminantia*,
which he says may be considered as an order very distinct of the
Mammalia—the first class into which vertebrate animals are divided.
—*"* The order of the Ruminantia is characterized by its cloven feet, by
the absence of the incisors to the upper jaw, and by having four
stomachs." The identity of definition is immediately perceived ; for
though in the quotation we have just made, Abarbanel only indirectly
refers to the four stomachs of the ruminants, yet in other passages
of his writings they are specially referred to as characteristics, just
as they are in the Talmud. See in particular the Treatise *Cholin, Perek
Elu Terephot, &c.*, p. 42. The absence of such reference, however,
in the above passage from Abarbanel, leads us to observe that the names
given in the Talmud show how intimate the ancient Hebrews were,
even before the destruction of the second temple, with the mechanism
and philosophy of rumination. In the first place, we remark that
with reference both to position and functions, the first and second
stomachs have much in common. Thus, though at first sight, the
second stomach would seem to be merely an appendage to the third,
in front of which it is; yet, it may, with greater propriety, be
regarded as rather a prolongation of the first. This first stomach, which
is the largest, is named the *paunch* (magnus venter rumen, aut, penula)
is covered with papillæ and is lined by a layer of the epidermis ; and
the second which is called the honeycomb [reticulum arsineum] from
the mucous membrane which lines its interior, forming a multitude
of folds so arranged as to constitute polygonal cells, like those of a
bees comb. And with reference to their functions, recent investigation
has shown these to be *identical* in respect to the regurgitation by which
the food contained in them returns into the mouth. For this has mostly

been attributed to the second stomach only, whereas it is now established especially by the experiments of M. Flourens, that both the first and second stomachs are instrumental therein. * Moreover food remains in both, until after a second maceration, when it passes on to the third and fourth stomachs. From all this is very apparent the propriety of the Hebrew term which is one and the same for both stomachs, viz.: בית הכוסות Beth hakossoth the cup-like or celular regions † the word כוס generally translated cup, referring either to the stomach being a hollow vessel to receive matter, to be poured therefrom again, as is certainly the office of the cup, more especially when, as of yore, the grape (vegetable matter) was pressed into it for the refreshment of the guests at the wine feasts; or else referring to the papillæ of the internal surface of the first, as of the polygonal cells of the second. The third stomach called *many plies*, on account of its large longitudinal leave-like folds, in Hebrew, receives the names of המסס Hamesses, from which the Latin name for the third stomach *omasum*, we think is unquestionably derived, wherefore it needs to make no further remark thereon. ‡ The fourth stomach is called *reed* (abomasum faliscus ventriculus intestinalis) and in Hebrew קיבה (Kebah) which is derived from the root נקב (Nakob. See Parkhurst thereon) meaning to perforate, and conveying, as will be seen, the same idea as the English term. From this brief analysis is evident, as we imagine, that the ancient Hebrews were well acquainted with the mechanism of rumination, and, it would be reasonable to conclude, as a conse-

---

* " By their contraction," Dr. W. B. Carpenter informs us, " the paunch and honeycomb force the alimentary mass which they contain between the borders of the furrow of the œsophagus, and this contracting in its turn, takes up a portion of it, separates it, and forms it into the ball which is destined to return along the œsophagus.

† *Kos* in Talmudical Hebrew also means a pore. Vide Lingua Sacra, Rad. Kos.

‡ Save that the Aruch in a comment on the word as occurring in the Talmud has the following remarks "מסס ובית הכוסות *Messes* and *Beth Hakossoth* signify the stomach, because the concoction of the food therein, is called *Messes* like the passage והיה כמסס נסס [This passage Isaiah x. 18, is translated in the English version, " and they shall be as when a standard bearer fainteth". Without examining the correctness of this rendering, we state that the root *massos* means to melt, and the connexion between this idea, and that of the functions of the *omasum* is very clear.] The Aruch then shows how the word has been explained by others, which, as not immediately concerning us, we pass over. The following note to the Aruch, added by R. Benjamin Musaphia, an author of the highest order, we give in full, as it confirms what has been advanced above with reference to the terms applied to the stomach—הומסוס בלשון רומיי אחד מן קרבי הבהמות המעלות גרה וכלל זה יעלה בידך כל הבהמות הטהורות יש להן ג כרסים ולריאה שלהן יש אונות נם לכבד שלהן יש אונות והכליות שלהם מחותבות לא כן הבהמות הטמאות כי כדם א לדם והריאה וכן הכבד והכליות חתיכה א כל א מהם וכנגד הג כרסים שיש לבהמות הטהורות יש נם ג כרסים לעוֹפות טהורות זפק וקרקבן וכרס א קטן נם לדנים הטהורים יש כרסים :

quence, with the phenomena and process thereof also. Continuing now our comparison between the definitions of Abarbanel and Cuvier, let us premise this single remark. It is not to be forgotten that neither the Talmud nor Abarbanel are writing medical or physiological treatises, yet, the latter gives what none can consider a contemptible account of the process of rumination as compared with those of modern writers. A further remarkable identity in Abarbanel's and Cuvier's definitions is easily and clearly perceivable by comparing the last two paragraphs of the quoted comment with the following postulates of the renowned naturalist in his formal and learned treatise :—" A hoof which envelopes all that portion of the toe which touches the ground, blunts its sensibility, and renders the foot incapable of seizing." "For cutting flesh, grinders are required as trenchant as a saw, and jaws fitted like scissors which have no other motion than a vertical one." "Hoofed animals are all necessarily herbivorous, and have flat crooked grinders, inasmuch as their feet preclude the possibility of their seizing a living prey, &c., &c."

We continue Abarbanel's remarks having reference to the general directions for discrimination laid down by the Levitical law. "Our pious sages have traditionally supplied us with the signs whereby we may distinguish the clean from the unclean of those ruminant animals possessing horns. Beasts which ruminate, having no grinders or incisors on the upper jaw are supplied by nature with horns ; the matter which should form these teeth being compensated by her with horns, which renew after their birth, at which time they do not possess any." This teaching is thus verified in one of the most recent and popular works on Zoology, that of Dr. Carpenter. "Horns are found on the heads of all the other animals of the order, in the males at least. The horns essentially consist of prominences of the frontal bone. * The Mammalia which are furnished with bony branching horns, all belong to the order of the Ruminants." † Abarbanel continues, "The use of these horns to such animals is that they may defend themselves therewith against casualties and attack, since they cannot fall back upon their teeth and claws like the predaceous animals." Our commentator then proceeds to discourse of the distinguishing signs of birds and fishes, which we must omit for the present, while we see what further has been advanced by Hebrews respecting the clean animals.

Maimonides in his Yad Hachasakah, at the first chapter of his Treatise on Forbidden Meats, which contains the Hebrew traditional signs of discrimination, &c., writes as follows :

* Sec. 259.   † Sec. 52.

§ 1. "It is an affirmative precept [obligatory on Israelites] to become acquainted with the signs which distinguish between beasts, domestic and wild, birds, fishes and locusts. [The word employed by Maimondes is חגבים (Chagabim) which, though we translate locusts, rather means the *Orthoptera* and *Saltatoria* of modern naturalists] permitted or prohibited for food, as it is said, 'ye shall make a distinction between the beast which is clean and that which is unclean, and between the fowl which is unclean and that which is clean.' It is also said, 'make a difference between the unclean and the clean, and between the beast that may be eaten and the beast that may not be eaten, (Lev. xi. 47.

§ 2. The distinguishing signs of domestic and wild animals are explained in the Levitical law, and are two, both 'dividing the hoof' and 'chewing the cud;' every ruminant animal hath no teeth or incisors in the upper jaw; and every ruminant beast also divideth the hoof, the camel excepted ; and every beast which divideth the hoof cheweth the cud, the swine excepted. * § 3. Therefore, he who finds

---

* The great Cabballist, Harabad (R. Abm. ben David) attacks this definition of Maimonides, briefly referring to the cases of the *Shafan* * and the *Arnebet*. The attack is, however, groundless and unjust, as it would appear, since Maimonides, though writing in the 12th century, writes like the great philosopher he was, just, as we have seen above, Cuvier in our age writes when discoursing of the Ruminantia of which animals *as an order or class*, Maimonides correctly speaks. He is ably defended, however, by the author of the *Magid Mishneh* who says : "From what our teacher (Maimonides) himself writes elsewhere, as well as from the explanations of Holy Writ, we know that the *Shafan* and *Arnebet* ruminate, but divide not the hoof. It is also known that it (the *Arnebet*) hath teeth, incisors, in the upper jaw, as the Talmud informs us, but with this our Rabbi was of a verity well acquainted, the proper interpretation of his words being this, Having already explained that clean beasts require both signs, his expression ' every beast which ruminates. &c.,' refers to the clean animals, which is indeed the case. as is shown in the Talmud which affirms—' You cannot find any of the clean animals which are ruminant that have incisors in their upper jaw.' Our author then explains that every ruminant animal, i. e., that also does not possess incisors on the upper jaw, divideth the hoof, the camel excepted, as is further explained in the Talmud, which says, ' The camel approximates to the clean animals in respect to its ruminating and in its want of the regular number of upper grinders. * * It is also stated in the Talmud, that the camel has ניב (niboe) on the upper jaw, meaning two teeth, proceeding different ways at the extremities of the cheeks. The same authority also informs us that the young of the camel have not their teeth developed but are like the clean animals in this respect. It would appear then, that our author writes in a manner having reference to these ancient Talmudic teachings, intimating that the camel, which is ruminant, is at the same time peculiar *sui generis*. None ruminating is unclean, like the camel, [there being also a peculiarity of hoof in its case] therefore is it particularly mentioned in the text. Harabad thought, however, that our teacher intended to assert, that all ruminant animals had no incisors on their

*The nomenclature of these animals is a subject for after consideration.

a beast in the wilderness and is ignorant of its nature, but finds its hoofs divided; he examines its mouth, and if it has no teeth above, then it is undoubtedly clean; and thus is the camel distinguishable. If he find a beast with incised or fissured mouth, he examines its hoofs, if they be divided, it is clean; and thus is the swine distinguishable. If he finds both mouth and feet cut, he examines it, after it is slaughtered, beneath the backbone. [On tearing the flesh, in this part of the female camel, some of it will rend woofwise, and some warpwise:—Rashi,] if he find its flesh proceed [or tear] warpwise and woofwise it is clean, and so is the ngarood distinguishable, for such is the nature of its flesh. [The "ngarood" is generally translated *wild ass*, Job xxxix. 5. It denotes the same in Chaldee with some variation in the form, as it is used in the plural, which is not the case in the Hebrew. It is also so understood in Talmudic Hebrew. See Keleem ch. viii., the Aruch, and Ling. Sac. rad. Arod. In Shemoth Rabba, sec. 1, fol. 149, it denotes a species of serpent.] § 4. A clean beast that begot young having the appearance of an unclean animal, although it divides not the hoof, and chews not the cud, but is like the horse or ass in every respect, this young is permitted for food, that is, when born in the Israelite's presence; but if he should set apart in his flock a cow which is with young, and after an absence, finds a young one like the swine, even if it suckle it, it is yet doubtful and prohibited for food, for possibly it may have been born of an unclean animal, though attaching itself afterwards to the clean. § 5. An apparently clean beast, begotten of an unclean beast, although it divide the hoof and chew the cud, and is even in all respects like an ox or like a sheep, is yet unlawful food; since a preponderance of the unclean, we must pronounce as unclean, and of the clean, we must consider as clean; wherefore an unclean fish, found within one clean, is prohibited; and a clean fish found in one unclean, is for the stated reason, permitted. § 6. A clean beast that begot, or that contained, a creature [monstrosity] having two backs, and also a double back bone is prohibited food; this is the שסועה [Shessungha, cloven, or divided] to which holy writ refers, when it declares, [Deut, xiv. 7.] 'Nevertheless, these ye shall not eat, of them that chew the cud or of them that divide the פרסה השסועה [Parsah Hassesbungha, cloven hoof,'] implying a creature that was born, being divided or parted, as it were. into two animals. § 7. And so with respect to any beast in which

---

upper jaw, hence his correction; the result, however, is to show that all animals possessing regular incisive teeth are unclean. He (Harabad) further thought, that it was the intention of Maimonides when he wrote that 'every ruminant animal divided the hoof' to convey, that this is so in respect both to those who do and do not possess such teeth; but I have already explained his opinion."

was found a creature, having the form of a fowl; although it may prove one of the clean species of fowl, yet must it be accounted as unlawful food. It is not proper to regard as clean, any creature found in any animal but such as possess hoofs. § 8. Of all beasts, wild and domestic, which the world affords, none are permitted for food except the ten kinds specified in the law.* Three are of the domestic kind, viz.: 1. שור [shor, ox; we retain, for the present, the translation of the Anglican version,] 2. שה [seh, sheep] 3. עז [ngez, goat]; and seven are included among the wild beasts, viz: 1. איל [ayal, hart] 2. צבי [tsebi, roe-buck] 3. יחמור [yachmur, fallow deer] 4. אקו [ako, wild goat] 5. דישון [dishon, pygarg] 6. תאו [tèo, wild ox] 7. זמר [zemer, chamois] these and their various genera, such as the שור הבר [shor abar, according to some the wood-ox. Compare Targ. Jer. Ps. l. 10. Treat Peah ch. 8, Rashi, Ps. l. 10, according to others the תרבלה Tarbelah wild ox or buffalo; Targ. Onk. Deut. xiv. 5. Cholin fo. 80, a.] and of the מרי [merie, translated by some, fatted ox] which are of the ox kind. All these ten species and their genera, are ruminant, and of bifurcated hoof; therefore, he who [at first sight] knows them, need not examine either their mouth or feet, [to ascertain their lawfulness for food.] § 9. Although they are all permitted for food, yet do we require to discriminate between the clean among domestic, and the clean among wild animals; for the fat of the wild animal is permitted, and its blood, [issuing at the time it is slaughtered] must be covered; whereas with respect to

---

* "It was well known and manifest before him, who ' said and the world was' that the unclean animals exceed the number of the clean; therefore doth holy writ enumerate the clean; and also that the clean fowl exceed in number the unclean, therefore doth the text enumerate the unclean"—Talmud, Treat. *Cholin, Perek Elu Terephot*, P. 63., b. See the *Magid Mishneh*, which cites this passage, and one further (page 80, of the same treatise,) to show that Maimonides is correct in the traditional rule he lays down as to the number and division of the enumerated animals. There is a discussion—particularly interesting with reference to the knowledge of natural history displayed—as to the correctness of Maimonides' classing the *shor habar*, (generally understood as the wood-ox) among the wild beasts, upon which subject there is a difference of opinion in the Talmud; but it is too lengthy, for more than a passing notice. Its importance in fixing a charge of apparent self-contradiction on Maimonides, is but very small, since it can with truth be asserted, that he writes with reference to the opinions contained in the Talmud, as indeed the *Magid Mishneh* gives us good grounds for believing;—besides modern naturalists have disputed upon similar points, and it is not always profitable or necessary, to repeat the grounds of their opinions. The inquiring reader, will find this discussion on reference to the *Magid Mishneh*, the *Keseph Mishneh*, and other commentaries, published with the *Yad* of Maimonides, also to the Talmud, Treatise *Kilaim, Perek Oto Vëet Beno*, &c. We learn however, that the *shor habar*, is, according to some, identical with the תרבלה *Tarbelah*, Wild ox, or Buffalo, (see Targ. Onk. Deut. xiv, 5, *Cholin* fo, 80, a.) while according to others, it is of the goat kind.

the domestic animals, the sacrificial suet is prohibited under pain of excision, and its blood does not require to be covered. § 10. The distinguishing signs of the wild beasts, are supplied to us by tradition. Thus, every animal dividing the hoof, and chewing the cud, and possessing divided horns like the איל (ayal, stag,) is to be considered as unquestionably clean; but with reference to all, not having their horns divided, if their horns be covered or encased, like the horns of the ox, incised like the horns of the goat, and the incision erased, and crooked like the horns of the tsebi [roebuck,] these are wild animals which are clean, provided always that the horns possess these requisites, being encased, incised, and crooked. § 11. This applies, however, only to such kinds of animals as are not known; but as to the seven species of wild beast mentioned in the law, if one be well acquainted with these, even if he find that they possess not horns, he may eat its fat, and is obliged to cover its blood in slaughtering it. § 12. The *shor habar* is of the domestic species, and the קרש *keresh*, [by some translated, unicorn] although it possess but one horn it is accounted as a wild animal. All, respecting which, there may be a doubt as to whether it be of the wild or domestic class of animals, the fat of such is prohibited, the scriptural penalty of stripes is not incurred, and the blood thereof is to be covered at the time of slaughtering. § 13. A beast of mixed breed produced from a domestic animal that is clean and a wild beast that is clean is called כוי (kooi) its fat is prohibited, the penalty of stripes is not incurred, and they cover its blood." Thus far Maimonides as to the distinctive signs of beasts.

A further result of a critical examination of the text would be to establish, secondly, as regards *fishes*, that "whatever hath fins and scales in the waters, in the seas and in the rivers," are to be accounted clean and proper for food, and as such, may be used by the Hebrews; whereas " all that have not fins nor scales in the seas, and in the rivers," adds the text, v. 10, " of all that move in the waters, and of any living thing which is in the waters, they *shall be* an abomination unto you. v. 11. They shall be even an abomination unto you; ye shall not eat of their flesh, but ye shall have their carcasses in abomination. v. 12. Whatsoever hath no fins nor scales in the waters, that *shall be* an abomination unto you." This is further shown by the Hebrew writers, to whom we have just referred. Abarbanel's remarks are as follow—"Just as two conditions characterise the clean beasts, and two, the clean fowl, [Abarbanel refers here to his comment, respecting the clean birds which we omit till hereafter] so doth the text lay down two conditions which must be possessed by the clean fishes. Its expression, therefore, is, "these may you eat of all that are in the waters, all that have fins and scales in the waters, &c.," but those

which are not so characterised "shall be an abomination unto you."
Some have thought to assign as a reason for these directions, that
fishes that possess fins and scales, are enabled to swim to and fro
wherever and whenever they desire ; whereas those who do not possess
fins and scales, are not so able; wherefore they [the latter] remain continually in muddy places in the water, and become earthy and of
unwholsome nature. But this is in reality not the case, for fins and
scales are engendered in fish, in consequence of a superflux of nature
which they possess, and therefore doth their body become clean and
good for food, which is not the case with those not possessing fins and
scales. These latter are of an exceedingly moist nature, and have not
the advantage of getting rid of this natural superflux, which is, as it
were, shut up with them, and therefore is it that they are pronounced
unclean. The text adds with reference to these fishes the expression
"in the seas and in the rivers," because there is a vast difference
between those found in salt water and those in rivers of fresh water,
and therefore doth it lay down one general rule for all, and establisheth
one law for all that move in the waters, and for all living things in the
water, whether you conclude them to be of the reptile or fish species.
The word שקץ [shekets, an abomination] is employed three times in
the text, and the expression "all that have no fins nor scales" twice,
because there are some fish which possess scales while they are in the
water, but leave them there when taken forth from the water. The text
therefore says explicitly, "all that have fins and scales *in the waters,*
both in the seas and rivers, these may you eat, but those which have
no fins nor scales while they are in the seas and rivers, you of your
own accord shall loath and abominate as things to be rejected of men ;
and even as they are abomination unto you because of your natural
antipathy to them, so shall they become one in consequence of this
command. Ye shall then not eat of their flesh, nor touch their carcase
for they shall be an abomination [shekets]. The word שקץ [shekets],
is derived from and compounded of אשר [asher, which] and קץ [kats, to
vex or fret] as in Genesis xxvii, 46, קצתי בחיי, I am vexed or fretted
[Ang. vers. weary] with my life." Now because some might peradven-
ture say, 'Not to eat of them is, doubtless, proper, since their
flesh is bad; but as to the penalty attached to touching them, why
should their carcase be pronounced an abomination ?' on this account
saith the text for the second time, 'all that have no fins nor scales in
the waters shall be an abomination unto you'; as if it were giving us
the Talmudic caution במופלא ממך אל תדרוש [Investigate not matters
above your comprehension] and seek not of yourselves to assign reasons
for my commandments. As sum of all, take this general rule,—All

aquatic and marine creatures which do not possess fins and scales, shall be an abomination unto you, and this, whether in respect of eating or touching them."

The very important caution which Abarbanel cites as to subjecting any of the precepts of holy writ to a presumptuous system of ratiocination, he most certainly does not mean to apply to any inquiries into the nature of the animals permitted or prohibited, since we have seen, and shall yet further see that he himself enters deeply and ably into this subject; and, moreover, particularises the *how* and *where* such an investigation becomes improper or reprehensible. In proceeding, then, to examine presently, the directions of the Levitical law with reference to the birds, we shall dwell for some time upon the analogy existing between the clean birds and the clean quadrupeds, which we think well worthy of notice, and intimately connected with our subject. At present we have to inquire what the other eminent Jewish authority, already quoted, teaches with respect to the permitted and forbidden fishes. Maimonides devotes one paragraph (the twenty-fourth) of the chapter from which we have before translated, to a notice of the distinctive signs of fishes; it is as follows:—" Two signs distinguish the clean fishes, fins* and scales; the former enable them to swim, and the latter cleave all

---

* It may be necessary here to continue our examination of the text. We notice first, מים *Mayim* and ימים *Yamim*, the waters, " from the root ים *yam*, tumult. As a N. masc, plur; (it has a dual termination,) thus denominated from their being so susceptible of, and frequently agitated by, tumultuous motions,"—Parkhurst. Wessely in his comment on the 11th chap. of Leviticus, says " The word *mayim* applies to all waters, those of seas, rivers, ponds, and of pits, caves, &c., and even those which are contained in utensils of any sort; for fish can multiply in all, therefore is the word *mayim* used here indefinitely, so as to imply all fish that breed in the water. *Yamim* means the oceans, as it is said ' the gathering together of the waters, God called *yamim*.' * * * *Nechalim* means those streams (rivers) which are the products of the rains and springs, alluded to in Ecclesiastes i, Ps. 104."

סנפיר *Senaphir* means, according to all, *fin*, and is therefore correctly rendered in the Ang. version and by the Spanish translators as *ala*, by the German, *flossfedern*, *cauda pinna piscis*. Targ. *tsits*. The LXX. have *Pterugia*, wings, probably from the resemblance maintained between it and the wing of a fowl.

קשקשת *Kasskeset* scales; *escama*, "literally, a little piece, so called from its rigidity,"— Park. "*Kasskesset* means the skinny portion fixed to the fish, as in 1 Sam. xvii. ' with a coat of mail (shiryon kasskassim) he was clad;' so writes Rashi, but Nachmanides remarks that these scales cannot be said properly to be fixed to the fishes' skin, but are round integuments which can be removed with the hand or knife, wherefore it is said in the Talmud that *kasskesset* is a dress, * * for as a dress is quickly put off, so may these scales be easily removed with the hand; but this is not so with those which cleave to the skin, [and which circumstance establishes such fishes to be unclean]."—Wess.

E

over their bodies. All possessing fins, possess scales. If they do not possess these in the first instance,* but they afterwards grow with them, or if they have scales whilst in the water, but when drawn forth, they leave them in the water, they are permitted. Those which have not scales covering the whole of their bodies are permitted ; indeed, though they had only one fin and one scale, they are permitted." To these remarks it may, perhaps, be added as worthy of note, that fish with fins being only permitted, there is, so to speak, a connecting analogy herein exhibited between these and the just mentioned superior animals (quadrupeds) which those fishes not possesing fins, most certainly do not exhibit ; and whereby, it is perhaps not unreasonable to suppose an inferiority in these finless and scaleless fishes, in respect to their approaching to aquatic or marine *reptiles,* is implied by the sacred penman. This opinion may be considered as deriving some support from the circumstance that naturalists have uniformly remarked upon the analogy existing between the organs of locomotion of fishes, and those of quadrupeds ; thus, the fins of the former, called the *pectoral* or thoracic, from their situation, have been considered as correspondent with the fore feet of the latter ; and those placed farther back called *ventral* or abdominal fins, have been conceived to represent the hind feet of the first class of vertebrated animals. The vertical fins on the back are termed *dorsal* fins, and those on the under surface of the body *anal* fins ; the fin by which the tail is terminated being termed the *caudal* fin. The membranes of these fins are supported by rays or bands more or less numerous, and those of the pectoral and ventral fins, according to the represented analogy between the organs of fishes and quadrupeds, have been supposed

שקץ *skekets* an abomination, particularly what is ceremonially unclean ; specially applied to reptiles.

שרץ *sherets* a reptile, worm ; *sherets hangoff* winged reptile, lesser fishes. " The Paraphrast must have concluded this word to mean, particularly, movement, for he translates it רחשת"—Kimchi. Abarbanel says it is compounded of *asher* which, and *rots* runneth. " *Reptile, omne animal quod supra terram non eminet, terrestre aut aquatile ut sunt ranæ, locustæ formicæ, crabrones, vermes et pisces,* Gen. 20." " The *moving things,* or as the Greek translateth *creeping things.* But the Hebrew *sherets* is more large than that which we call the creeping thing, for it containeth things moving swiftly in the waters as *swimming fishes,* and the earth, as running *weazels, mice, &c.* R. Salomon on Exod i., saith that they did bring forth six at one birth. [Rashi says this because of the extraordinarily rapid increase of the Israelites in Egypt, the word in the text being *vayishretsu*], and Aben Ezra, that the women brought forth twins and more." Critica Sacra.

* The Yoreh Deah explains (ch. 83, §1, *comment*) that if the scales cannot be removed readily with the hand or any other instrument, they are not to be accounted as such, and the fishes are to be pronounced, in consequence, unclean.

to represent the toes of the feet. From hence, also, is apparent the expressiveness and propriety of the Hebrew term for *fin* which is סנפיר a pluriliteral, compounded of סנה (Seneh) *a thorn*, and פר (Par) *to break*, and of Parkhurst's remark that " the frame or texture thereof gives the reason of the Hebrew name," since the fin of a fish consists of *rays*, or according to the Hebrew phrase, of *thorns i. e.*, little *bones* or cartilaginous ossicles supporting a membrane *broken* or divided into several partitions. Those who would see the analogy ably carried out would do well to refer to Professor Stark's valuable " Natural History," (Ed. Edinb., 1828, v. 1., p. 377,) from which we cannot refrain transcribing his following brief, but flattering, panegyric of our learned co-religionist Bloch. " Among those who contributed to that progress, (of Ichthyology, or study of fishes) by accurate representations of the animals, Mark Eleazar Bloch, a Jewish physician at Berlin, deserves to be noticed. His *Ichthyologie ou Histoire Naturelle des Poissons,* in six volumes folio, was published in 1785-95, with 452 colored plates, the greater part of which are accurately drawn and described from nature; and the facts connected with the history, specific differences, and uses of fishes detailed with equal accuracy, have furnished most subsequent writers with a storehouse of information on the subject of the European species. The original edition being difficult to be procured, a small copy in ten volumes, 18 mo, was published at Paris in 1801."

The distinctive signs of *birds* are not supplied us by the Scriptures, though they are by ancient Jewish tradition. In the Talmud, Treat. Cholin (Mish. ch. 3, § 6) we learn " that every [predaceous] bird which strikes its talons into its prey* is unclean : every bird which has an additional claw,† a crop, and of which the internal coat of the stomach may be peeled off [with the hand] is of the clean species. Every bird which [when placed on a perch] divides its toes equally, is an unclean one." Abarbanel when pointing out the means of compensation exhibited in the cases of the wild and domestic quadrupeds, which we have already quoted, thus continues his remarks which have refer-

* דורס *Doress*, according to some, such as do not wait for the death of their victim but eat it alive, and although the common fowl eats worms and reptiles while they yet have life, yet could not the Hebrew term *derisah* be properly applied to this.

† Placed behind and above the front ones; the toes are usually in number four, and never more numerous, sometimes of the external or internal finger one or both disappear, so that only three, as in the case of the Bustard or even two, as in the Ostrich remain. Three of the four toes are generally directed in front, while the fourth is turned backwards. In the family *Phasianidœ* or Pheasant tribe, the hind toe is placed higher on the tarsus than the front ones, so that only the tip touches the ground, and the tarsus of the male is generally furnished with one or more spurs; so in the common fowl.

ence to birds. "There are some of the predaceous birds having sharp claws, [talons] but not having an additional claw above their feet, whereas the feet of clean birds are extended according to the require- ment of their manner of walking to gather their food in the fields. They have, in consequence, an additional toe above their foot, that their pro- gress may be not impeded, just like those beasts which have their hoofs fully divided [are distinguished from the beasts of prey]. The clean birds have also a crop [פזי zephec] and a stomach, the internal coat of which may be peeled off [with the hand] for the re-grinding of their food. In this [preparing their food in the crop and gizzard] they are like unto those which ruminate among beasts, [who also require more than one stomach for the maceration of their food] The *ngorib* [raven] is [an exception to the rule among birds] as the swine [is among beasts] having only one of the necessary conditions, viz : an additional claw, and not being properly a predaceous bird, but it does not conform to the rule with reference to its digestive apparatus and the peeling of the stomach above mentioned. There are also of the unclean birds [presenting this contradictoriness] like the camel, *shafan* and *arnebet* [among beasts,] since if they exhibit one of the signs of the clean birds, they do not pos- sess the other ; hence the rule ' every predaceous bird is unclean.' Their nature is fierce and intractable, their temperament bad, being nou- rished by such food only as they hastily tear and swallow, and therefore are they prohibited."

The learned Abarbanel, whose elegant and valuable commen- tary we continue to select as the able expositor of Jewish tra- dition affecting the points we are discussing, in the just com- pleted extract, continues to show the remarkably correct acquaintance which the ancient Hebrews had with natural history, more than twice ten centuries since. The admirable adaptation of the feet to the nature and wants of each of the two classes of birds, is, evidently, insisted upon by our author with singular propriety. The reader will please compare his remarks with those in the note on p. 53. He states that an iden- tity exists in the ruminating and digestive apparatus of the clean beasts and the clean birds. For that general reader who may not have paid special attention to the fact, we venture to exhibit the following com- parison. The œsophagus in birds beginning at the inferior part of the neck communicates with the first digestive cavity named the *crop*. This first stomach corresponds to the first and second in the *Ruminantia*, viz : the *paunch* and *honeycomb*, (we have shown that for good reasons these receive only one name in Hebrew, and are in more than one respect, iden- tical, even if the second be not a mere appendage of the third stomach, as some have thought). The food remains for a time in this crop.

Below it, the œsophagus is again contracted, and presents further down a second dilatation, called the *ventriculus succenturiatus*, whose internal surface is perforated by a considerable number of small pores. This again corresponds with the *many plies* of the ruminating beasts, and opens below into the *gizzard*, in which the process of chymification is completed. This corresponds with the *reed* of ruminant beasts, and in birds that feed on flesh only, its sides are thin and membranous, but in those that swallow food which is harder and more difficult to digest, it is furnished with strong muscles intended to compress and to grind down its contents. Its inner surface is covered with a sort of almost cartilaginous epithelium. Our commentator refers to certain exceptions to the rule, but to these remarks, pertinent and correct as they are, it will be proper to refer, when considering the nomenclature of the animals. The following observations of Dr. Carpenter in his interesting work on Zoology, will, however, be in itself confirmation sufficiently strong of Abarbanel remarks. " It is impossible not to recognise the obvious analogies between the different groups of Carnivorous Mammalia, and those of the predaceous birds. The bold and powerful eagles obviously resemble the lion and other large felines; the smaller and yet more sanguinary falcons correspond with the smaller felines and with the mustelidœ; the cowardly carrion-feeding vultures resemble the hyœna and wild dog; whilst the owls may be likened to nocturnal viverridœ; we shall find that there are certain species, aquatic in their habits, and which are parallel, therefore, to the otters and seals."* Abarbanel thus continues his comment, " Fishes are mentioned by the sacred penman after beasts, because like the latter, they have assigned them two distinctive signs of legality, but which birds have not ; those to which I have already alluded, being according to the tradition of our pious sages, upon whom be peace. These signs of the clean birds are, moreover,

* We are forcibly reminded here of Dr. Paley's remarks in his chapter on *compensation.* " It has been proved by the most correct experiments that the gastric juice of these birds (granivorous and herbivorous) will not operate upon the entire grain, not even when softened by water or macerated in the crop. Therefore without a grinding machine within its body, without the trituration of the gizzard, a chicken would have starved upon a heap of corn, yet, why should a bill and a gizzard go together ? Why should a gizzard never be found where there are teeth ? Nor does the gizzard belong to birds as such. A gizzard is not found in birds of prey. Their food requires not to be ground down in a mill. The compensatory contrivance goes no farther than the necessity. In both classes of birds, however, the digestive organ within the body bears a strict and mechanical relation to the external instruments for procuring food. The soft membranous stomach accompanies a hooked, notched beak : short muscular legs; strong sharp crooked talons; the cartilaginous stomach attends that conformation of bill and toes, which restrains the bird to the picking of seeds or the cropping of plants."

internal, whereas [to correspond with the cases of beasts and fishes], they should be external, so as immediately to be recognized. The law therefore does not refer to these signs, but mentions the unclean species of birds, the clean being the most numerous. Those birds which are not specified in the text as prohibited, rank under the category of the permitted. In Dueteronomy, Moses, we find, particularises the clean beasts permitted for food, while of fowl he says, ' all clean fowl ye may eat,' in general terms."

The following is the Jewish law of discrimination for birds according to Maimonides in the 1st chapter of his Treatise on Forbidden Meats already referred to. " § 14. The signs of the clean birds are not explained in the law ; but it lays down the number of unclean birds, and all others are permitted. The prohibited are twenty-four in number, and may thus be enumerated. 1. נשר [nesher, generally translated as in the Anglican version, eagle]. 2. פרס [peres, ossifrage]. 3. עזניה [ngosniyah, ospray]. 4. ראה [daah, vulture], which is identical with the ראה [raah, Ang. vers. glede] of Deuteronomy. 5. איה [ayah, kite] identical with the דיה [dayah Ang. vers. vulture] of Deuteronomy. 6. A species or order of the *ayah* ; for it is written in the text ' its kind,' also, from which is established that there are two kinds. 7. עורב [ngoreb, raven]. 8. זרזיר [zarzir, generally understood as a stare or starling, Baba Kama fol. xcii. 2] for it is said, 'the raven after its kind,' to include hereby the zarzir. 9. (בת) יענה [yanganah, owl]. 10. תחמס [tachmass, nighthawk]. 11. שחף [shachaf, cuckow]. 12. נץ [nets, hawk]. 13. שרנקא [sharneka,] a species of hawk, as the text shows, from its employing the term, 'after its kind,' to the hawk. 14. כוס [kos, little owl]. 15. שלך [shalach, cormorant]. 16 ינשוף [yanshuff, great owl]. 17. תנשמת [tinshemet, swan]. 18. קאת [kaat, pelican]. 19. רחמה [rachama, gier-eagle]. 20. חסידה (chasidah, stork]. 21. אנפה [anafah, heron]. 22. A species of the *anafah* as stated in the text. 23. דוכיפת [doochifat, lapwing]. 24. עטלף [ngatalef, bat). § 15. Every one who is well acquainted with these various species and their nomenclature, may eat of every bird not included in this list, and without examination. Clean birds are eaten on the strength of tradition, it being of course a well established thing in the place where the bird is eaten, that such is a clean bird, and one experienced in hunting [and the names] of these birds gives his testimony to their being clean. § 16. He who cannot readily distinguish them, but is intimately acquainted with their nomenclature can examine them by these signs with which our sages have supplied us ; to wit, every bird that strikes its talons in its prey and then eats it, such, it is clear, is of the enumerated species, and is unclean ; if it does not this, however, it is yet clean, provided it possess one of these three signs, an additional toe or claw, or it possess a crop, or that the internal coat of the stomach can be peeled off with the hand. § 17. There is not among all these prohibited species any one that is not predaceous, and having one of these three signs, except the *peres* and *ngosniyah*, and the *peres* and *ngosniyah* are not found in inhabited places, but in deserts and very distant places, and at the utmost verge of civilization. § 18. If the skin of the stomach is removeable with a knife but not with the hand, and the bird [in such a case] has no other sign [of being unclean], although it may not strike its claws in its prey, yet is it a doubtful case. If the stomach be tough, and [the skin] cleave closely to it, but by being exposed to the sun, it becomes soft and easily peeled by the hand, then it is permitted. § 19. The Gaonim, [eminent Rabbis who flourished just after the completion of the Talmud] have declared that they have been traditionally cautioned against teaching the legality of a bird possessing only one sign of its being clean, unless that one sign were that the skin of its stomach was readily peeled with the hand ; but if this one sign obtain not, although the bird possess a crop or an additional claw, yet can they never permit it to be considered as clean. § 20. Every bird which divides [equally] its paws when placed on a perch, two one way, and two another ; or that he seizes [his food] in the air and there eats it, is undoubtedly of the predaceous kind and unclean; and all which associate with the unclean, and approximate to them [in nature and habits] are unclean." To this the Yoreh Deah adds, (ch. 82, §3), "Some assert that every fowl with broad beak and expanded, [palmated or webbed] feet like those of the goose, is well known to be non-predaceous, and is lawful food, provided it have the three signs. § 4. A person who happens to be from a place where they are accustomed to account as prohibited a certain fowl because they have no tradition, that it is clean, and he goes to a place where they have a tradition that it is of the clean species, he may eat thereof in that place, even if his intention be to return to the other place ; and if he went from a place where they pronounce it to be traditionally clean, and go to another place where they have no such tradition, he can yet eat thereof. § 5. Places having no tradition respecting the character of the birds, depend upon those which have, to eat thereof. Some prohibit and some allow, but it is preferable to abide by the decision of those who prohibit." Thus particular are the directions of the Jewish canon, respecting the means of discriminating the clean and unclean birds.

With respect to *reptiles* and *insects*, the law thus directs, " V. 20. All fowls that creep, going upon *all* four, shall be an abomination unto you. V. 21. Yet these may ye eat, of every flying, creeping thing, that

goeth upon *all* four, which have legs above their feet, to leap withal
upon the earth. V. 22. *Even* these of them ye may eat, the locust after his kind, &c. V. 23. But all other flying, creeping things, which have
four feet *shall be* an abomination unto you. V. 27. And whatsoever
goeth upon his paws, [kapav] among all manner of beasts, that go on
all four, these *are* unclean unto you; whosoever toucheth their carcase,
shall be unclean until the even. V. 29. These also shall be unclean
unto you, among the creeping things that creep upon the earth, the
weasel, &c. V. 42. Whatsoever goeth upon the belly, and whatsoever
goeth upon *all* four, or whatsoever hath more feet among all creeping
things that creep upon the earth, them ye shall not eat for they are an
abomination. V. 43. Ye shall not make yourselves abominable with
any creeping thing, that creepeth, neither shall ye make yourselves unclean with them, that ye should be defiled thereby." We cite Don
Isaac Abarbanel's comment upon this; he writes—" In addition to its
first stated instructions respecting birds, the text adds : ' all fowls that
creep going upon *all* four, shall be an abomination unto you,' because
there are creatures which now creep the earth like reptiles, and anon
fly in the air. All such, the text pronounces an abomination ; except the
mentioned four kinds of locusts [chagabim] which are permitted.—
These go on *all* four, and have legs above their feet,—feet higher than
the ordinary ones which they require to leap withal upon the earth ;
when they desire to jump, they effect it by these feet, raising their wings,
which cover the greater portion of their body. The distinguishing
signs of these locusts (chagabim) are, that they possess [extra] legs for
jumping [pedes saltatoria] four feet and four wings, which cover the
greater part of the body, and with a long head—to such is the term
chagab properly applied. It becomes us to ask here, why is it said
' and ALL fowls that go on *all* four, &c.' ? because, the text gives a general
rule with respect to all such, and would add, ' these species which I mention, ye may eat, and they do not come within the category of reptiles ;'
and so after specifying these, it adds, ' all the rest which go on *all* four,
shall be an abomination unto you, and shall not by any means be accounted among those of which I have said, even these of them ye may eat'.
After mentioning the creatures which may legally be eaten, and those
also which are unclean and are to be abominated, the text informs us of
those which render unclean all who *touch* them. When it says therefore,
' for these ye shall be unclean' (v. 24) it means for these which will
now be mentioned ; again the text saith, ' and whatsoever goeth upon
his paws, and every beast that goeth upon *all* four,' and not on his *hoofs*,
like the dog, bear, and cat, &c. • • • • It would seem that the
caution [repeated in the 41st verse] that every ' creeping thing, is an

abomination and must not be eaten,' is unnecessary, since it is already given, in a former part of the chapter, but its intent is to show that every reptile besides the eight mentioned above, are unclean and must not be eaten."

Rashi says, "all fowl that creep," [sherets hangoff, v. 20] alludes to those of the smaller and lower order of animals moving upon the earth, such as flies, gnats, locusts, &c. After giving the old Jewish traditional signs of those animals, which may be considered as *chagabim*, and which are quite identical with those given by modern naturalists to the *saltatoria*, Rashi adds " all these signs are to be found in those which come among us, but there are some having an extended head, but not possessing a tail, and yet belong to the species *chagab* [saltatoria] but thus, are we unable to discriminate correctly concerning them. In the 41st verse, there occurs the repetition, [to which Abarbanel also refers] because it implies as exceptions to the prohibition, such insects as are found in *kalisin*, [according to some a species of cedar-fruit or fig; according to others, pulse, Ter. fol. lix. Chol. fol. xvii. 2,] and the maggots in lentiles, which only when creeping upon the ground are prohibited. The expression ' whatsoever goeth upon the belly,' in verse 42, refers to the serpent.— The reduplication of the words ' that goeth, &c.,' in the same verse, shows that the *shilshulin* are to be here included. [This remark of Rashi, it should be observed, is like all we have quoted above as his comment, nothing more than national, traditionary teachings which we may find in the Talmud, chiefly in the treatise Cholin. This last of his remarks, is from this treatise.* R. Benj. Musaphia, in the M. Hearuch, show us that *shilshulin*, means a kind of worm.] " Going upon *all* four" adds Rashi, " refers here to the scorpion, and the repetition of the word ' all,' shows that the *cheepusheet* [black-beetle, Chol. fol. 67] called in French *escarbot*, is included, ' what hath more feet' alludes to the *nadal* [a reptile having many feet, Chol. fol. lxv., and Erub. fol. viii. 2, according to Mendelssohn, it is identical with the *Iulus* of Linnœus, of which more presently] and the word *sherets* again repeated here, we know to allude to a reptile which have feet [in equal succession] from head to tail, and, which is called *centpied* [centipede.]" Such is the explication of Rashi. In the Beraytah of Torath Cohanim, a very ancient commentary on Leviticus, it is explained, that the first " whatsoever goeth," in verse 27, refers to the monkey tribe, and its reduplication includes the *kofed* (bittern,) *choled* (weasels of the bushes,) and the *adnay hasadeh* [as some understand, wild men; others baboons, &c.] and the *keleb hayham*, sea dog, &c.," all of which are subjects for after remark.

* בסוף גמרה דפרק אלו טרפות בחולין ֹתֿני רבנן הולך על נחון זה נחש בל לרבות את השלשול ואת הדומה לשלשול

Maimonides after numerating the eight species of *chagabim* or locusts, proceeds to give the traditional signs, which establish them as such. § 22. He who is well acquainted with these and their names may eat of them, but he who is not, examines the three distinguishing signs, which they possess. All which have four legs and four wings, extending the greater part of the length and breadth of their body, and having more-over, two springing legs, is of the clean species; although its head might be long, and it had a tail, it is clean, so long as it is known to be of the species *chagab*. § 23. Such as have not yet wings or springing feet, or wings covering the greater part of their body, but [it is known] that they will obtain them hereafter when they are grown, then, even at such early state, they are permitted."

We have now shown the reader, perhaps at greater length than his patience might require,—but not more so, than was deemed necessary for a proper appreciation of the subject, what are the rules for discri-minating the clean and unclean of beasts, fishes, birds and reptiles, deemed authoritative by the Hebrew people ; and it becomes us now to pay some attention to the second point we have to discuss ; to wit,—the nomenclature and nature of the enumerated animals. For such of our readers, who may be interested in the subject, we shall take the pains to exhibit a large number of the very highest authorities, both ancient and modern, Jewish and Christian, because, necessarily a more correct opinion is thereby to be formed, and because they will establish one very important fact, with reference to the birds especially, which we cannot pass over. Our examination commences with the quadrupeds.

1. נמל (gamal) camel* v. 4. T. O. נמלא (Gamala,) "he cheweth the cud but di-videth not the hoof." S. J. T. and de R , camello; G. T. Kameel; M. id. ; B. camelus; D. L. and G. camel; F. camelus; K. id. ; C. S. id., M. A. id. "The root denotes retribution or return. As a N. a *camel* from the revengeful temper of that

---

* In the examination about to be made, the rendering of the English version will immediately follow the Hebrew name, while other authorities, for the sake of brevity will be expressed by the following initial letters. S. J. T. will mean Spanish Jewish Translators, de R. de Reyna, G. T. German (Christian) Translators, M. Mendelsohn, B. Buxtorf, F. Furst, D. L. David Levy, P. Parkhurst, G. Gesenius, M. A. Moosaph Hearuch, K. Kimchi, R. Rashi, Ab. Ez. Aben Ezra, Ab. Abarbanel, T. O. Targum Onkelos, W. Wessely, S. Serrano, C. S. Critica Sacra, Linn. Linnœus, Cuv. Cuvier, Carp. Carpenter ; and so with other authorities already referred to. Where no translation of the foreign names are given, they are the same as the Ang. Vers., so also, when they are omitted.

Serrano observes that the Spanish names by which he translates the text, are, except in such cases where tradition has decided, only applied because of their composition and roots representing the characteristics and qualities of the animals whose names he employs. The same is remarked by Wessely before giving a translation to the birds. "We are not familiar and cannot be assured of their names, so I follow the old commentators, some of whom were also in doubt on the matter. Thus I do not lay down the law as a decided thing ; but it was necessary to translate them."

animal, which Bochart shows to be so remarkable as even to become a proverb among those nations who are best acquainted with its nature. Among other passages from ancient writers, he cites from Basil. 'But what marine animal can emulate the camel's resentment of injuries, and his steady and unrelenting anger ?' The reader will be well entertained by consulting the excellent and learned Bochart himself on this animal, v. ii. &c."—P. " It is not the case with the camel that his foot is covered with a shoe-like hoof, and so with the *shafan* and *arnebet*, and therefore the text cannot and does not add the words 'and is cloven footed ;' but in the case of the swine who does possess such cloven foot the words are used,"*Compare v. 7.—W. " The camel's foot is divided into two distinctly marked toes, although not positively cloven, which are fastened to, and rest upon, the elastic pad or cushion at the end of the foot. From this circumstance, it has been a nicely balanced question whether the camel, which chews the cud, can be reckoned among the species called cloven-footed. It seems to be a connecting link between those that are and those that are not."--Pict. Illus. Bib. A peculiarity of stomach is also noticed by Buffon. " Independent of the four stomachs which are commonly found in ruminating animals, the camel is possessed of a fifth bag which serves him as a reservoir to retain the water. The fifth stomach is peculiar to the camel, &c." " Water is constantly retained from the great masses of cells which cover the sides of their paunch, the other ruminants have nothing of the kind—Cuv. Order vi. Bisulca (Pecora Lin) Gen. xxix.—Stewart. It is without horns and of the order Ruminantia."—Stark, &c. R. Ab. Ez. and Ab.--the same. Where such unanimity of opinion exists we cannot but see the correctness of the Aglican version..

2. שפן (shafan) coney, "he cheweth the cud but divideth not the hoof;" T. O. טפזא (tapza) ; S. J. T. & de R., conejo, which also means rabbit. G. T. & M. Kaninchen ; B. cuniculus, mus montanus ; D. L. & G. coney ; F. mus jaculus Linn.; Sept. Choirogrullios. K. id. C. S. id. " The dry, hot nature of the Shafan is well known," Ab. "It is accustomed to resort to concealment in rocks, as it is said, ' the Shefanim are but a feeble folk, yet they make their houses in the rock.' Again in Ps. 104, 18. The word ' divideth' is in the Hiphil form, participle when applied to the camel, in the future tense to the coney, and to the hare in the préterite, which may be meant to teach this. Do not think that those born without dividing the hoof will hereafter do so, for the text couples the ' not' with the future tense ; or that it may have had a divided hoof which is now not distinguishable, for the text joins another ' not' with the past tense."--W. " The meaning of the root Shafan is to cover in, conceal. As a noun Shafan means a kind of unclean animal, so called from hiding itself in holes or clefts of

* R. Wessely, from whose Hebrew comment this is an extract, next condemns the learned Rashi for his translation of *Parsah*. We do not think that it is at all neces sary to prolong such an inquiry, having already fairly given Wessely's reasons for dissent. For our part we do not think the great Rashi's remarkable acuteness and research has at all failed him. He can in this matter be very easily defended, and were this the place, even we would make an humble attempt so to do. We respect Wessely as a classical Hebrew scholar and able grammarian, but we cannot help feeling that in common with but too many modern Jewish critics, especially with his countrymen--while they display much ingenuity—they are but too apt to forget that if different premises are set up, in criticising some of the old *Mepharashim* very different conclusions will be arrived at. We repeat that the translation of Rashi, we think, every way correct and every way defensible by a mere tyro. But nothing is more probable than that an expression should be differently understood by different parties.

rocks. Ps. civ. 18, Prov. xxx. 26. In the second edition of this work, I followed
Bochart's interpretation of *Shafan* by the Jerboa, *i. e.* the *Mus Jaculus* or jumping
Mouse; but I am now inclined to embrace Dr. Shaw's opinion, that it signifies the
Daman Israel, or Israel's Lamb, 'an animal, says he (Travels, p. 348), of Mount
Libanus, though common in other parts of this country [namely Syria and Pales-
tine]. It is a harmless creature, of the same size and quality as the rabbit, and
with the like, incurvating posture, and disposition of the fore-teeth. But it is of a
browner colour, with smaller eyes, and a head more pointed, like the marmot's. As
its usual residence and refuge is in the holes and clefts of the rocks, we have so far
a more presumptive proof that this creature may be the Shapan of the Scriptures,
than the Jerboa, which latter he says, p. 177, he had never seen burrow among
the rocks, but either in a stiff loamy earth, or else in the loose land of the Sahara,
especially where it is supported by the spreading roots of spartum, spurge—laurel,
or other the like plants. Mr. Bruce likewise opposes the Jerboa's (of which he has
given a curious print, and a particular description in his Travels, vol. v. p. 121), being
the Shafan of the Scriptures, and thus sums up his observations on this subject, p.
127. ' It is the character of the Saphan given in the Scripture, that he is gregarious.
that he lives in houses made in the rock, that he is distinguished for his feebleness,
which he supplies with his wisdom. (See Prov. xxx. 24, 26, and Ps. civ. 18 in Heb).
None of those characteristics agree with the Jerboa: and, therefore, though he
chews the cud in common with some others, and was in great plenty in Judea so
as to be known to Solomon, yet he cannot be the Saphan of the Scripture. And in
a following section Mr. Bruce contends that this is no other than what is called in
Arabia and Syria, Israel's Sheep [the Daman Israel of Shaw] and in Amhara,
Ashkoko, of which animal also he has given a print, p. 139, and a minute description, and thus applies to him, p. 144, the characters just mentioned. 'He is above
all other animals so much attached to the rock, that I never once saw him on the
ground and from among large stones in the mouth of caves, where is his constant
residence: he is gregarious, and lives in families. He is in Judea, Palestine and
Arabia, and consequently must have been familiar to Solomon.—Prov. xxx. 24, 26,
very obviously fix the Ashkoks to be the Saphan, for the weakness here mentioned
seems to allude to his feet, and how inadequate these are to dig holes in the rock,
where yet, however, he lodges. These are perfectly round: very pulpy or fleshy,
so liable to be excoriated or hurt, and of a soft fleshy substance. Notwithstanding
which they build houses in the very hardest rocks, more inaccessible than those of
the rabbit, and in which they abide in greater safety, not by exertion of strength,
for they have it not, (for they are truly as Solomon says a *feeble folk*.) but by their
own sagacity and judgment, and therefore are justly described as *wise*. Lastly,
what leaves the thing without doubt is, that some of the Arabs particularly Damir
say, that the Saphan had no tail: that it is less than a cat and lives in houses, that
is, not houses with men, as there are few of these in the country where the Saphan
is: but that he builds houses, or nests of straw, as Solomon has said of him, in contradistinction to the rabbit, and rat, and those other animals that burrow in the
ground who cannot be said to build houses, as is expressly said of him.' Thus Mr.
Bruce: and for farther satisfaction I refer the reader to his account of the Jerboa,
and Ashkoko. I add that Jerome, in his epistle to Sunia and Fretela, cited by Bochart, says the Shefanim are a kind of ' animal not longer than a hedge-hog, resembling a mouse and a bear.' (The latter, I suppose, in the clumsiness of its feet).
Whence in Palestine it is called *arktomus* q. d. the *bear-mouse ;* and that there is

great abundance of this genus in those countries, and that they are always wont to dwell in the ' caverns of the rocks, and caves of the earth.' This description well agrees with Mr. Bruce's account of the Ashkoko. And as this animal bears a very considerable resemblance to the rabbit, with which Spain anciently abounded, it is not improbable, but the Phenicians might, from Saphan, call that country Saphania. Hence are derived its Greek, Latin and more modern names : and accordingly, on the reverse of a medal of the Emperor Adrian, (given by Scheuchzer, tab ccxxxv.) Spain is represented as a woman sitting on the ground with a rabbit squatting on her robe."—P. " That the shafan cannot be identified with the coney or rabbit is very plain. The rabbit is not an Asiatic animal, and it is very far from being solicitious of a rocky habitation, which is the distinguishing characteristic of the *Shafan* mentioned in Prov. xxx. 26. Some, therefore, suppose the Jerboa to be intended. * * The general accuracy of Bruce's account has been attested by more recent observations. It is so much an animal of the rock that Bruce says he never saw one on the ground or from among the large stones at the mouths of the caves, &c., in which it resides. * * They certainly chew the cud as the Shafan is said to do in Lev. xi. 5." " They are wise in their choice of habitations peculiarly suited to their condition, and they might be particularly mentioned in this view from the fact that animals of the class to which they belong, are usually inhabitants of the plains. The flesh of the Shaphan was forbidden to the Hebrews : and in like manner the Mahometans and Christians of the East equally abstain from the flesh of the *Daman*." Pict. Illus. Bib. " There is a curious genus of small animals inhabiting the rocky districts of Africa and Syria which is intermediate in its character between the Tapir and Rhinoceros, but presents several points of resemblance to the Rodentia. This is the Daman or Hyrax, an active fur-covered little animal ; something called the Rock-Rabbit, and probably the Cony referred to in the Book of Proverbs. Its skeleton closely resembles that of a Rhinoceros in miniature, and its molar teeth are formed in the same manner : the feet have four toes, which are tipped with hoof-like nails, whilst the hind feet have three ; of which the innermost is furnished with a long claw-like nail. The best brown species are the Cape Hyrax, which inhabits Southern Africa: and the Syrian Hyrax of Syria, Arabia, and Abyssinia. Both these are active, hairy animals, somewhat larger than Rabbits, living in families, and taking up their abode in caves or crevices in the sides of rocks ; they live upon the young shoots of shrubs and upon herbs and grass, and they are playful in their habits, and docile and familiar in captivity." According to the same authority the Jerboa is an intermediate link between the Squirrels and Rats, it is distinguished by the enormous developement of its hind legs and tail, resembling the kangaroo. It is a native of Syria, &c., known to the ancients under the name of Dipus. Stewart ranks the Jerboa among the Digitata, and says it burrows in the ground. We have, however, made this investigation much longer than proper for the limits we should set down. The result of an extended inquiry, has led us to adopt the opinion that the *shafan* is identical with the *Daman* or *Hyrax*, and although this is now classed by the most respectable naturalists, among the order *Pachydermata*, which as an order of the Mammalia do not ruminate, yet is it to be remembered that the same authorities show us that the ordinary *Pachydermata* (under which the Daman is classed) " approximate the Ruminants in various parts of the skeleton, and even in the complication of the stomach" and " the stomach of the Damans is divided into two sacs; their cæcum is very large, and the colon has several dilatations, and is also furnished with two appendages about the middle analogous to the two cœca of birds," see Cuvier, *Règne Animal.*

3. ארנבת (arnebet) hare, v. 6, "he cheweth the cud, but divideth not the hoof." O. ארנבא (arneba). S. J. T. and de R. liebre; G. T. and M. haase; F. lepus; Sept. dasipous; all *hare*. "From ארה (arah) *to crop*, and ניב (nib) *the produce of the ground*—the hare—these animals being very remarkable for destroying the fruits of the earth. Bochart who gives this interpretation of the word, excellently defends it by showing from history that hares have at different times desolated the islands Leros, Astypalœa and Carpathus. See his works, vol. ii. 63 and 995."— P. "The hares," says Cuvier, ' have a very distinctive character in their superior incisors being double; that is to say, there is another of small size behind each of them."—This is identical with the old Talmudic definition to which we have already referred, on p. 46. Although placed among the *Rodentia* by modern naturalists. it is to be observed that the partial division in its stomach (see Carpenter's Zoology, v. 1, p. 268) would well warrant its classification among the *Ruminantia* where the text places it.

4. חזיר(chazir) swine, v. 7. "he divideth the hoof and is cloven footed, yet he cheweth not the cud." T. O. חזירא (chazayra) S. J. T. and de R. puerco; G. T. and M. schwein; B. and F. porcus. "The root means to encompass. As a N., a hog or boar, so called; perhaps, from his round shape when fat, which is his natural state; *Totus teres atque rotundis*."—P. Order *Pachydermata*. We shall have reason to speak of the nature and habits of the swine, when inquiring into the third point of discussion laid down. We now pass on to the birds.*

1. נשר (nesher) eagle, v. 13. T. O. נשרא (nishra) S. J. T. and de R. aguila; G. T. and M. adler; B. and F. aguila; D. L. and G. eagle. "The root means to lacerate, tear in pieces. The eagle species is eminent for rapacity and tearing their prey in pieces, for which purpose they are furnished with beaks or talons remarkably strong."—P. "The assertion of our sages that the eagle has no additional claw, has been attacked, but I, myself, have examined one, found in my native place, and found

---

*In Leviticus, twenty species of unclean birds are enumerated, while Deuteronomy specifies twenty one. We cite the following reconcilement of the apparent contradiction from the "Conciliator" of R. Menasseh ben Israel, Mr. E. H. Lindo's translation. "In Siphrè (which is adopted by Rashi) it says, in solution of this doubt, that the difference between Leviticus and Deuteronomy consists in the former saying ואת הדאה ואת האיה 'And the vulture and the kite and their species,' whereas Deuteronomy has it והראה ואת האיה והדיה למינה. Here the raah is named, which is not in Leviticus; there is also another difference in Deuteronomy, saying, *dayah* instead of *duah* as in Leviticus, the *yod* being in place of the *aleph* which being considered, it says that ריה איה דיה *Raya, Aya, Daya,* are all the same species of bird, but having various appellations from their different properties; so that there is no difference between the two passages, one only having an additional name, although of the same species. The difference between the words *dahh* and *raah* is nothing, for the Hebrew language admits this change of letter. (See note on question, 132.) The learned Aben Ezra says, that *raah* is the denomination of the genus which includes the different birds mentioned, whereby the objection is also answered, for the *raah* mentioned in Deuteronomy, is not a distinct species, but the name of the genus. This author avails himself of what is said of the patriarch Abraham, when, by the command of God, he took ' a young heifer, a goat, a ram, a turtle dove, and pigeon.' The scripture relates that he divided all in two, except the bird called צפור (which is applied to birds generally) and in that place, it is used instead of תור (a turtle dove,) which was mentioned before. R. Levi Ben Gershon holds that *daah* and *raah* is the same bird which from being sharp sighted and flying quickly, had both names given it in Hebrew, signifying those two properties, *raah* being derived from the verb *raah* ' to see,' and *daah* from the verb *daah* 'to fly,' and Deuteronomy, to avoid error, and for greater perspecuity enumerates both, without, however, adding another species, and he understands *dayah* and *ayah* to be the same, being commonly called by both names: so the verses thereby agree."

that it had no such additional claw."—W. The eagle is classed by Cuvier among the *Accipitres* or birds of prey, which are, he says, like the *Carnivora* among quadrupeds. "They are pre-eminent for their strength," adds Carpenter, "and attack not only birds for their prey, but the smaller quadrupeds also, such as the hare, sheep, fawns, roebucks, &c."

2. פרס (peres) ossifrage. T. O. ער (ngar) S. J. T. and de R. azor ; G. T. habicht (hawk or goss hawk, also of the order *Accipitres*) M. beinbrecher and small black eagle ; B. and F. ossifraga. "Peres is a large bird found rather in deserts than inhabited places, and R. Yonah, saith that it is identical with the Arabic *Akab*."—K. The root means to break, hence the remark of the Critica Sacra "withstrength of beak or talons she breaketh her prey ; *nomen est avis magna quœ deserta incolit, inquit R. David, ab ungulis fissis dictœ. Alii accipitrem, vel aquilœ genus putant. Alii Gryphum malunt. Ita Septuaginta Chald. & Vulgat. vertunt.*" "As a noun a species of eagle called by the Romans *ossifraga* or *bone breaker*, because he not only devours the flesh, but even breaks and swallows the bones of his prey. Comp. Mic. iii. 3 ; and see Bochart, vol. iii. 186, &c."—P. "According to most of the translators, it means a kind of eagle."—W. Order Accipitres, Cuv.

3. עזניה (ngosniyah) ospray ; T. O. עזא (ngasya) S. J. T. esmerejon (martin, also the yellow-legged falcon, *Falco Elesalon* Linn. Order Accipitres) G. T. fischaar, fischadler (sea eagle) M. schwarzen adler (black eagle) B. Haliœetus, (species aquilœ). F. aquilœ species, a visus perspicacitate (Job 30;29). Crit. Sac. haliœtus, a marine eagle, so called from its sharp vision, *quia adversus solis radios intueri potest*, Plin. l. 10. c. 3, "called the black eagle, according to Bochart, from its great *strength* in proportion to its size. * * The Targum renders it *ngasya* [strong one] and so preserves the idea. * * Bate, Crit. Heb. explains it by the *whining kite*, from ניח *neyah* its noise and עז *nges* impudent, strong and bold disposition and in his note on Lev. xi. 13, he says they have on the South Downs in Sussex, a whining kite which may be heard when very high in the air. * * Whatever bird was intended, I think it was so named from *nges* its strength, and *niyah* its moaning."—P. "Pandion haliœêtus. Some think the black eagle is here intended, but the probabilities are at least equally in favor of our version."— Pict. Illus. Bib. Order Accipitres, Cuv.

4. דאה (daah) vulture, v. 14, T. O, דיתא (dita) S. J. T. milano (glead kite) *falco miloris* Linn. G. T. Geier ; M. Weissen habicht (white hawk) B. milvus. "Vulture, changed in Deuteronomy into ראה probably through an error of the copyists"—F. "Primary meaning flight, the bird is so called from the extreme rapidity of its flight"—K. "The kite is called in Hebrew, Lev. 11, 14, *Daah* of flying, Deut. 14, 13, *Raah* of seeing, for the kite flieth with violence, and espieth her prey from farre."—Crit. Sac. "A kite or glead, so Vulg. milvus, which is remarkable for flying, or, as it were, sailing in the air with expanded wings. Thus our English glead is from the v. to glide, &c,"—P. Order Accipitres, Cuv.

5. איה (ayah) kite ; v. 14., T. O. טרפיתא (tarapheta) S. J. T. bueytre, G. T. meihe M. Schwarzen habicht (black hawk) B. carnix (crow, rook.) "An unclean predaceous bird of the vulture species, probably so called from its cry,"—F. Crit. Sac. cornix. "A species of unclean bird, remarkable for its sharp sight. See Job xxviii, Lev. xi, 14, Deut. xiv, 13. In the first passage, the English translation renders it a vulture, in the two latter, a kite, I should rather think it means a vulture and that this bird was so called either from its ravenousness, or, from the cry it makes,"—P. "In Deuteronomy, the text has ' the raah, and the ayah and the dayah after its kind.' Our sages affirm (in Cholin, folio 63. that the raah and daab

are identical, as are the ayah and dayah ; and according to R. Abuah (loc. cit) the daah, raah, ayah and dayah, are merely different names for the one bird, * which is called raah, which in Hebrew means to see, because of its *quick sightedness* ; and from its rapid *movement*, the expression moving, ' as the eagle,' being proverbial and the ayah may also be thus called, [for the word *ayeh* means *where* in Hebrew and the exclamation *ayeh* is the most likely to rise to the lips when this bird is in flight, since it is so soon lost in view. These qualities are more particularly found in that bird which in German is called *habicht* (hawk)"—W. "It is so called because it is accustomed to frequent known places (eyim)"—Ab. Ez.; Milvus, Order, Accipitres, Cuv.

6. ערב (ngoreb) raven, v. 15, T. O. עורבא (ngoorba) S. J. T. cuervo ; G. T. and M. raben ; B. and F. corvus. The root means to mix, hence the following remarks of Bochart and Aben Ezra. "The color of a crow or raven is not a dead, but a glossy shining black like silk, and so is properly a mixture of darkness and splendour." "It is of the same signification as ngereb, i.e., evening, implying mixture," "Order Passerinæ " It scents carrion at the distance of a league, and also feeds upon fruit and small animals, even carrying off poultry," Cuv.

7. בת היענה (bat hayanganah) owl, v. 16, T. O. בת נעמיתא (bat nangameta, S. J. T. hyju del autillo, Ser. and Cass. de R. abestruz (Strix Aluco, Linn.) G. T. strauss (ostrich) B. ulula. "It resides chiefly in desert places, and has a lugubrious cry"—K. " Ostrich, so called from their loud crying to each other. ' In the lonesomest part of the night,' says Dr. Shaw, ' they frequently made a very doleful and hideous noise which would sometimes be like the roaring of a lion ; at other times it would bear a near resemblance to the hoarse voices of other quadrupeds, particularly of the bull and ox. I have often heard them groan as if in the greatest agonies, &c. &c. &c. See the continuation of Parkhurst's interesting remarks on Lam. iv. 3, etc. Rad. ענה " Aben Ezra on Exodus xxiii, 19, writes, that the flesh of the yanganah is dry as wood, that men eat it not, because of its lack of moisture, but the young female's is eatable as possessing some. The additional word *bat*, our sages say, refers to the egg of the yanganah." " Some say that the *bat* [meaning daughter or young female] *hayanganah* present a species in which there is no male found ;—that the word in the plural has a masculine termination, is nothing, since we find it frequently applied to femenine nouns, e. g. yangalim, rechalim,"— Ab. Ez. There is certainly a female Ostrich, wherefore Ab. Ez. cannot refer to them. Cuvier classes the owls among the Accipitres and the ostriches among the Grallœ or stilt birds, which "feed upon fish, reptiles, worms and insects."

8. תחמס (tachmass) night hawk; T. O. צץ (tsitsa) S. J. T. mochuelo (horn-owl) strix otus, Linn. G. T. nachtcule; M. schwalbe ; " So called because he violently pursues other birds seizing them for his prey, thus the Targum Yerushalmi translates it *chatuofitu*"—K. The root means violence, rapine. " The LXX. render it glauka and Vulg. noctuam. I think, therefore, it was some kind of owl, and considering the radical import of its Hebrew name, it might not improbably be that which Hasselquist, Travels, p 196, describes as " of the size of the common owl, and being very ravenous in Syria, and in the evenings, if the windows are left open flying into houses and killing infants, unless they are carefully watched, wherefore the women are much afraid of it."—P. " Some say it is the male of the bat hayanganah."—M. " Schwalbe, it is of the predaceous kind; some consider it to be the faclon, and this

name well becomes it, from its comparative fierceness among birds."—W. "From the root *chamas* violence."—Ab. Ez. Order Accipitres, Cuv.

9. שחף (shachaf)cuckow; T. O., צפור שחפא (tsippor shachafa) S.J. T., cerceta (or garceta, like Cass. de R. and Ser. widgeon, a kind of small wild duck *Anas querquedula* Linn). G. T., kukuk ; B., larus (sea mew). " Larus; according to Kimchi, a bird laboring under phthisis." So Furst translates shachafat. " Œsalon Jun. accipitris species, circulus, rather the cuckow. Pagnine rendereth it Phthitica."—Crit. Sac. " The sea gull or mew, thus called on account of its leanness, slenderness or small quantity of flesh, in proportion to its apparent size. LXX caron, Vulg. carus. " It is of the same signification as *shachafat* and implies atrophy, consumption ; the bird is an exceedingly thin one."—Ab. Ez. Cuvier places the cuckoos among the Scansores (climbers). " The cuckoos have a lax stomach, cœca like those of the owls and no gall bladder."

10. נץ (nets) hawk; T. O., נצא (natsa) S. J. T., gavilan (sparrow hawk, *Falco Nisus* Linn.) G. T. and M., sperber (sparrow hawk). B., accipiter. " From the root נץ (nitsats) *to fly*, so called, according to Aben Ezra, the Baal haturim and Shelomoh Yitschaki, from its being so constantly on the wing."—F. " It is a bird with which men hunt, and it will return to the hand of its master."—K. Crit. Sac. Accipiter; " It occurs in Cholin Per. El. Ter. where it is translated like Rashi by the French word *autour* (gashawk)."—M. H. " The hawk, from his rapid flight, or shooting away in flying ; occ. Lev. xi. 16, Deut. xiv. 15, Job. xxxix. 26, which last passage seems to refer to the migration of the hawk towards the south, for most of the genus of hawks are birds of passage."—P. " When its plumage is ample, it is constantly on the wing, and flies southward for heat."—Ab. Ez. Order Accipitres, Cuv.

11. כום (kos) little owl ; T. O. קריא (karya) S. J. T. balcon, (falcon hawk. Falco Linn.) G. T. kauzlein ; M. huhu ; B. bubo ; F. pelican ; a bird having a cup-like appendage to the craw." " R. Selomoh explains it by the foreign word, falcon, which resides with men, and is employed by them in hunting."—K. " Targ. and in Mas. Nidah it is translated *karia* and *kephupa*, and Rashi explains it as a bird , which cries during the night, and having something human about the appearance of its face. Compare Ps. cii. 6."—W. Perhaps the Kos is identical with the Lilith (Isa. xxxiv. 14) which is no doubt the *bubo maximus* or eagle owl. In the travels of Captains Irby and Mangles, the following observation occurs in their account of Petra. " The screaming of eagles, hawks, and owls which were soaring above our heads in considerable numbers, seemingly annoyed at any one approaching their lonely habitation, added much to the singularity of the scene." Order Accipitres, Cuv.

12. שלך (shelach) cormorant ; T. O. שלילונא (shaliluna) S.J. T. and de R. gavista, gavia, (sea-gull, gull, *larus* Linn.) G. T. schwan ; M. fischreiher (heron) B. mergus. "According to the Gemara, a bird that draws up fish from the water [Chol. fol. lxiii, 1,] LXX, katarraktes ; Vulg., mergulus,"—F. " Cormorant is so named in Hebrew of *shalach*, of casting itself down into the water"—Ainsw. ap. Crit. Sac. " Root means to cast; as a N. a kind of sea fowl, the *cataract* or *plungeon*. Its Heb. and Greek names are taken from a very remarkable quality, which is, that when it sees in the water, the fish on which it preys, it flies to a considerable height, then collects its wings close to its sides, and *darts down* like an arrow, on its prey. See Bochart vol. iii, p. 278, and Johnston Nat. Hist. de Avibus p. 94, who adds that by thus darting down it *plunges* a cubit depth into the water whence evidently, its English name *plungeon*,"—P. " Under the common appellation *shalach* the shag and some other species of *Phalacrocurax* or *cormorant* were included." Pict. Illust. Bib. where

F

ʀᴄᴄ a most interesting account of them. "As conveyed by the Targumist, a bird drawing fish from the water"—R. "Some say a bird that is accustomed to cast its young"—Ab. Ez. "Order Palmipedes (having webbed toes) their voracity is proverbial," Cuv.

13. ינשוף (yanshoof) great owl ; T. O., קיפופא (kifufa) S. J. T., lechuza (stirix passenina Linn.) G. T., huhu ; M., nachteule ; B., noctua ; "According to Kimchi, a bird that flies or cries at night only (nachteule) so also the Targumist ; according to Aben Ezra a bird only flying at evening because it cannot bear the light of the sun"—F. "An owl or bat, because it flieth at twilight."—Crit. Sac. Parkhurst, however, says that this interpretation, so generally accepted among Jews and Christians, is very forced, and endeavours to show at length that the Ibis is meant ; but we think his position quite untenable, and this for the reasons he himself states. "Rashi says that the kos (little owl) and the yanshoof are called in French, chouette (screech—owl) and there is another species like it which is called hibou, (owl). Rashi does not mean to say here that the Kos and Yanshoof are one and the same species, but they are placed together in one verse because they are alike in respect to crying out at night."—W. Order Accipitres, Cuv.

14. תנשמת (tinshemet)swan ; v. 18, T. O., בותא (bavta) S.J.T., calamon(purple water hen) G. T., and M., fledermaus (bat) B., mouedula. "Yitschaki understands it vespertilionis, like the mouse that flies at nights (bats), and AbenEzra adds it is so called from the exclamation שם (shom) there ! made on beholding it, and thus does the Targumist render it bavta (and not cavta as in many readings). Nevertheless it appears to be a kind of marine bird, and so the Seventy render it ibis, porphurion sea fowl or swan, it is also the name of a four footed reptile, &c."—F. "Perhaps a species of owl so called from its breathing in a strong and audible manner, as if snoring, But as in both these passages, particularly in the former, it is mentioned among the water fowls, and as the LXX in the latter, appear to have rendered it by the Ibis (a species of bird not unlike the heron) and the Vulg., in the former by cygnum the swan ; it should rather seem to denote some water fowl, and that (according to its derivation) remarkable for its manner of breathing. And therefore I think the conjecture of the learned Michaelis (whom see, Recueil de Questions p. 221) that it may mean the goose which every one knows is remarkable for its manner of breathing out, or hissing when provoked, deserves consideration."—P. [according to our opinion, but very little] "It is the French ehauve souris, and like the mouse that flies at night ; and the tinshemet which is mentioned among reptiles is similar, and has no eyes, it is called talpa"—R. "Swan, order Palmipedes, Ibis order Grallœ. The sacred Ibis, was adored by the Egyptians because it devoured serpents, &c."—Cuv.

15. קאת (kaat) pelican ; T. O., קאתא (kata) S. J. T., cernicolo, Cass de R., cione (Falco Tinunculus Linn.) G. T., rohrdommel (bittern) M., pelican ; B., platea, pelicanus. "A bird of the waters or desert which regurgitates what it swallows in its hunger (pelican). "R. Judah saith in the Talmud that the kaat is identical with the keek, and in the Jerusalem Talmud R. Ishmael teaches the same. In the Mishna there occurs the expression 'and not with the oil of keek.' (See Section Bamè Madlikin). And in the Gemara the question is put as to what is meant by the oil of keek ? which Shemuel answers by saying it is a water bird of that name."—K. "Platea avis, pelecanus, a vomitu. Conchas enim calore ventris coctas, rursus evomit, ut testis rejectis esculenta seligat ut scribit Plin. Lib. 10, cap. 40, et Aristol. lib. 9, cap. 10, de Histor. Animal, &c."—Crit. Sac. "Root ka to vomit ;—the pelican ; the principal food of the pelican or onocrotabus is

shell fish, which it is said to swallow, shells and all, and afterwards, when by the heat of its stomach, the shells begin to open, to vomit them up again and pick out the fish. See the continuation of Parkhurst's lengthy and interesting remarks under the cited root. This just quoted remark is verified, and we might say the very expressions found, perhaps unknown to him, in the Talmud Treat. Chol. p. 73, referred to by Aben Ezra and Wessely, in their comments. Order Palmipedes, Cuv.

16. רחם (racham) gier eagle; T. O., רקריקא (rakrayka) S. J. T., pelicano (Polecanus onocrotalus Linn.) M., specht; B., merops (bee catcher). " A bird of the vulture kind, so called from its love to its young, [its root means to have compassion, like *chasidah*, a stork from *chesed* mercy] vultur perenopterus Linn. The word used by the Targum has reference to its green color."—F. The remarks of Kimchi are embraced in the foregoing quotation from Furst. " Bochart, vol. iii. has taken great pains to prove that it means a kind of vulture which the Arabs call by the same names. So Dr. Shaw's Travels, p. 449, takes it for the *Perenopteros* or *Oripelargos* called by the Turks *Ach Bobba*, which signifies *white father*, a name given it, partly out of the reverence they have for it, partly from the color of its plumage : though in the other (latter) respect it differs little from the stork, being black in several places. It is as big as a large capon, and exactly like the figure which Gesner, lib. iii. De. Avib. hath given us of it. These birds, like the ravens about London, feed upon the carrion and nastiness that is thrown without the city of Cairo, in Egypt. In Lev. *racham* is placed between *kaat* the pelican and *chasidah* the stork, and in Deut. *rachama* between *kaat* the pelican and *shelach* the cataract, which positions would incline one to think it meant some kind of water fowl. But, however this be, this bird seems to be denominated from its remarkable tender affection to its young. Com. Ps. ciii. 13, Isa. lxiii. 15, 1 King's iii., 26."
—P. Order Accipitres, Cuv.

17. חסידה (chasidah) stork v. 19 ; T. O., חורירא (chavarita) S. J. T., ciguena (Ardea ciconia Linn.) G. T., and M., storch ; B., ciconia. " A bird exhibiting special compassion towards its young, [*chesed* means mercy or compassion] ciconia."—F. "We learn from Scripture that it is a periodical bird, or bird of passage, (Jer. viii. 7) that it has large wings (Zech. v. 9) and that it rests in *berushim* fir or cedar trees (Ps. civ. 17). All these circumstances agree to the stork which appears to have had the name *chasidah* from its remarkable affection to its young, and from its kindness or piety in tending and feeding its parents when grown old [the same derivation is given, in nearly the same words, by Rashi. See his comment.] I am aware that by some, this latter fact is treated as a fable, but I must confess when I find it asserted by a whole cloud of Roman and Greek writers, who had abundant opportunity to ascertain the truth or falsehood of it, and especially by Aristotle and Pliny, and that among the Greeks in particular, it passed into a kind of proverb in their application of the V. *antipelargein* and of the names *antipelargia* and *antipelargesis* for requiting ones parents, and in their calling laws enforcing this duty *pelargikoi nomoi*—on these authorities, I say, I cannot help giving credit to the fact just mentioned. * * * Chasidah cannot mean the *heron* for the common heron is not a bird of passage. It has, however, so great a resemblance to the stork that it is ranged by naturalists under the same genus. * * * They will feed upon frogs, carefully selecting the toads, which they will not touch."—P. But for its extreme length we would produce the whole of Parkhurst's learned and interesting article —we recommend the attention of the critical reader to it. Aben Ezra says that it appears at regular periodical intervals, as it is written Jer. viii. 7. " Yea, the stork in the heavens knoweth her appointed times, &c." " So punctual are they in their

comings and goings, that, from the most remote times they have been considered as
gifted with reasoning powers. • • The coming of the storks was the period of
another Persian festival, announcing their joy at the departure of winter. The expression 'the storks in the heavens' is more applicable than at first appears, for
even when out of sight, its path may be traced by the loud and piercing cries peculiar
to those of the new as well as of the old world. • • Besides the Jews, other
nations held this bird in veneration."—Pict. Illus. Bib. " Their gizzard is slightly
muscular and their two cœea so small as to be barely perceptible. Order Grallœ,"
—Cuv.

18. אנפא (anafah) heron ; T. O., אבו (eboo) S. J. T., ensanadera; Cass. de R. and
Serr., cuervo marino ; G. T. and M., reiher ; B., milvus (kite). " According to the
Talmudic doctors, the angry dayah or vulture, the root being *anaf* to be angry."—F.
" In Latin *Ardea* of *ardeo* to burn, chiefly because she is an angry creature." Crit.
Sac. " Heron, so named from its angry disposition, as the stork is called *chasidah*
from its kindness. Bochart, vol. iii. 337, takes anafah for a kind of eagle or hawk,
but if this were the true meaning of the word, I think it would have been reckoned
with one or the other of those species in the preceding verses."—P. " As in
Cholin the angry Dayah ; to me it appears to be the heron."—R. " *Anafah* because it becomes quickly incensed."—Ab. Ez. " Their stomach is a very
large sac, but slightly muscular, and they have only one minute cœcum. Order
Grallœ, Cuv.

19. דוכיפת (doochifhat) lapwing ; T O., נגר טורא (nagar toora, " cock of the moun-
tains." Elias in Methurgaman observes that it is called in German an *awrhane*. D.
L.) S. J. T., gallo montes ; Serr. and de R., aborilla ; G. T., miedehopf; B. upupa
picus " According to another opinion it is derived from *duch* (gallus) and *kefa*
(mons)."—F. " Rab. Sherira the Gaon, explains it also, to mean *tarnegol habar*
(wood cock). " The lapwing is so called of the double combe that it hath, *Gallus
sylvestris* aut *Gallina sylvestris*."—Crit. Sac. " The upupa, hoopoe, or hoop a very
beautiful, but most unclean and filthy species of bird which is, however, sometimes
eaten. So the LXX, *Epoph*, and Vulgate *Upupa*. (See Boch. v. iii. Brookes Nat.
Hist. v. ii. p. 123.) It may have its Hebrew name as it plainly has its Latin and
English one, from the noise or cry it makes."—P. " Wood-cock, its comb is double
in French *hupe*, called nagar toora, because of its acts, as our sages explain in
Masechet Gittin (p. 63)."—R. " The Sadduces say this is the cock, but they are
the fools of the world [most irrational,] for who told them ? [since they reject traditionary teachings.]"—Ab. Ez. Lapwing Order Grallœ, Cuv.

20. עטלף (ngatalef) bat ; T. O., עטלפא (ngatalepha) S. J. T., morciegalo ; G. T.,
schwalbe, B., vespertilio. " According to Aben Ezra, a small bird flying at night,
derived according to Kimchi, from ngatal (darkness) and ngef (to fly). This, however, does not seem a proper explanation to me. I consider it to be a reptile which
is like a mouse (bat) thus we find in Isaiah it is joined to *chefor perot* (ch. ii. v. 20).
(Ang. Vers. moles,) its root *ngatalef*, as in Latin talpa ; if so the *ngain* becomes para-
gogic, whence is derivable the bird's name which is like it."—F. " The winged
mouse which flies at night."—K. " Vespertilio quœ in caligine volitat, et interdiu
se velat."—Crit. Sac. " Perhaps from ngat to fly and ngalaf obscurity. A bat,
which flies abroad only in the dusk of the evening and in the night, according to
Ovid, Metam. lib. iv. fab. 10, lin. 415. Nocte volant, seroque trahunt,
a vespere nomen' "—P. "R. David Kimchi writes that it means the winged mouse
that flies at nights. If so, we find that the sacred book commences its enumeration
with the king among birds, viz : the eagle, and finishes with that which is intermediate

between a bird and a reptile"—W. Cuvier places the bats among the Carnaria, the third order of Mammalia.

Of *flying reptiles* (sherets hangof) we have mentioned 1. ארבה (arbeh) rendered by the Anglican version, locust; 2. סלעם (solngam) bald locust; 3. חרגל (chargole) beetle; 4. חגב (chagab) grasshopper. This first is translated *locust*, but the other three are left untranslated by the Spanish Jewish Transla*ors, Cassiodoro de Reyna, most of the German translators and Mendelssohn. They are rendered by Buxtorf, respectively, locusta; species attelabum; cantharus; and locusta; by Furst, locusta; species locustæ a *voracitate* nominatæ; genus locustæ, a saliendo, &c.; locusta gregaria. According to Kimchi, 1. locust; 2, one of the species of locusts, the רשון rashon (bald locust) of our sages [see Chol. fol. 65 a, and Vayikra Rabba, sec. 14] it has a bald forehead, no tail, but elongated head. 3. Species of locust; 4, the same. Parkhurst thus renders them, with the following remarks: 1, a locust; some place the word under this root, (arab) to lie in wait, because these insects suddenly and unexpectedly come forth upon countries as from *lurking* places plundering and destroying, &c., 2. from *salang* to cut, &c., a kind of locust, probably so called from its rugged craggy form as represented in Scheuchzer's Physica Sacra tab. ccl, fig. 1 which see, &c., 3. a kind of locust; it appears to be derived from *charag*, to shake, and *regel*, the foot, and so to denote the nimbleness of its motions. Thus, in English we call an animal of the locust kind, a grasshopper, the French name of which is likewise *sauterelle* from the V. *sauter* to leap. 4. * * I should rather think that *chagab* denotes the cucullated spicies of locust, so denominated by naturalists from the *cucullus*, cowl or hood with which they are naturally furnished, and which serves to distinguish them from the other birds, &c." P. The Arabs eat them in a fried state with salt and butter; and the writer of this has seen several Jews from Barbary eat the locust with much apparent gusto in the city of London, evidently considering it a great luxury, and themselves, much favored in being able to procure these native delicacies where the public taste has not yet called for them, though it requires, in abundance, creatures of most loathsome appearance and character, which it cannot, in justice, be said, the locusts present, The locusts are classed by Cuvier among the Insecta, 2nd family of the Orthoptera, viz: the Saltatoria.

With respect to *reptiles*, it will be seen from an examination of the word שרץ (sherets) on page 52, to which the reader is referred, that in Hebrew this word has a much wider acceptation than in English, and includes things moving swiftly in the waters, as *swimming* fishes, or on the earth, as weazels, mice, &c. This premised, the scriptural classification will be better appreciated.

1. חלד (choled) weasel v. 29, T. O., חולדא (choolda,) S. J. T., comadreja, (mustela vulgaris, Linn.) G. T. and M., wiesel; B., mustela; F., talpa, called so in the Talmud, because of its digging or scooping; we find " the Eternal hollowed for them (machlid) the earth."—F. K. mustela, " The weasel is called in Hebrew *choled*, of *cheled* time, not because it liveth long as *oleaster*, but because it soon waxeth old and so giveth way to time."—Crit. Sac. " It seems to have its Hebrew name from its *insidious creeping* manner."—P. " Order Carnaria (being very sanguinary, and living almost entirely upon flesh.) The true weasels are the most sanguinary of any"—Cuv.

2. עכבר (ngachbar) mouse; T. O., עכברא (ngachbera) S. J. T., raton; G. T. and M., maus; B. and F., mus. " Harmer shows that in latter days mice have been sometimes most destructive, to Palestine in particular"—P. Order Rodentia, Cuv.

3. צב (tsab) tortoise; T. O., צבא (tsaba) S. J. T., sapo; G. T., krote (toad,) M., schildkrote; B. testudo; " Bufo, à tumescendo, testudo,"—Crit. Sac. " The toad, from his *swelling* (the root means to swell) or rather because there seems no occasion to forbid eating the toad, the *tortoise*, from the turgid form of his shell"—P. " R. Eliau Bachur translates it *schildfrote* identical with *schildkrote*"—W. " *verdier*, approaching the frog", R.—Reptilia—Order Chelonia, Cuv.

4. אנקא (anakah) ferret, v. 30, T. O., ילי (yala) S. J. T., erizo (hedgehog) G. T. and M., igel; F., stellio, a sono. " So called perhaps from its continued cry"—K. " A kind of lizard or newt, so called from its moan or doleful cry"—P. *herisson* according to Rashi. Cuvier places the lizards among the Reptilia, second family of the Saurians. The lizards are distinguished by their forked tongue, &c. Those called the monitors frequent the vicinity of the haunts of crocodiles and alligators, it is said that they give warning, by a whistling sound, of the approach of these dangerous reptiles, and hence probably their names of *sauvegarde* and *monitor*"—Cuv. This is certainly intimated in the Hebrew name.

5. כח (koach) chameleon; T. O., כחא (kocha) S. J. T., lagartija; G. T., molch (salamander) B., lacerta, " genus lacertæ, non a robore nominatum, sed ab humare vel sputo quod emittit"—F. " R. Yonah writes that it is called *hardon*, it is a species of the צב (tsab,) and R. Solomon writes that in the vernacular it is called lizard."—K. " A species of lizard well known in the east, and called by the Arabs *alwarlo*, or, corruptedly from them, *warral* or *guaril*, and so remarkable for its vigor in destroying serpents and *dhabs*, (another species of the lizards) that the Arabs have many proverbs taken from these its qualities, &c."—P. " Rashi, Onkelos and Jonathan Ben Uziel and Mendelssohn do not translate this word at all; but it appears to me to be identical with the Arabic *guaril* known for its great strength." —W. Cuvier places the chameleons among the Reptilia, 5th family of the Saurians.

6. לטאה (letaah) lizard, T. O., לטאה (letaah,) S. J. T., caracol (snail) G.T., eider; B. stellio, lacertas, " lacertæ species, sic dicta quod terræ adhaereat (?)"—F. " A species of *poisonous lizard* called in Arabic *waehra*, and remarkable for adhering closely to the ground. Vulg, stellio, a *newt*, which may confirm the interpretation here given"—P. " The *lacerta gecko* is a species of lizard found in countries bordering on the Mediteranean, it is of a reddish grey, spotted with brown. It is thought at Cairo to poison the victuals over which it passes, and especially salt provisions, of which it is very fond. It has a voice resembling somewhat that of a frog, which is intimated by the Hebrew name, importing a sigh or a groan." Pict. Illus. Bib.—R. lizard. Reptilia, 2nd family of Saurians, Cuv.

7. חמט (chomet) snail, T. O., חומטא (choomta) S. J. T., babosa (limax, Linn,) G. T. and M., blindschleich (slow worm or snail) B., limax; F., limax ut plurimi vertunt. " Lacerta, secundum divum Hieron. vel limax. Testudo, cochlea terrestris secundum R. David."—Crit Sac. " A kind of lizard. In Chaldee the V. signifies to bow down, depress, prostrate; and the animal might be called by this name from its being (by reason of the shortness of its legs) always prostrate, as it were. In Josh. xv. 54, we have Chamta, the name of a town in Canaan, perhaps so called rom the *emblematic reptile* there worshipped, Comp. Deut iv. 8"—P. " limace"— R. Mollusca, Gasteropoda Pulmonea, Cuv.

8. תנשמת (tinshemet) mole; T. O., אשותא (ashota) S. J. T., topo, (talpa, Linn.) G.T. and M., maulwurf, B. and F., and K., talpa. " Root means to breathe as a N., a species of animal enumerated among the lizards. The learned Bochart hath plainly proved that it was no other than the *chameleon*, an animal of the lizard kind, furnished with lungs remarkably large, and so observable for its manner of *breathing*

or perpetually gasping as it were for breath, that the ancients feigned it to live only on the air. Thus Ovid, Met. lib. xv, fab. iv, lin. 411. ' Id quoque quod *ventis* animal nutritur et *aura*.' (The creature nourished by the wind and air)"—P. This applies equally to the mole, since " while employed throwing up those little domes which are called mole hills, he is said to pant and blow as if overcome with the exertion"—Pict. Illus. Bib. Yet the context would show that he is right in placing the *tinshemet* among the lizard species. Cuvier places the mole among the Carnaria of Mammalia.

From the foregoing analysis, we may consider the following as legitimate deductions. First, as regards *beasts*, we find that even such of them as approximate so closely to those which ruminate and divide the hoof, that the most able of modern naturalists have been in doubt as to their classification (e. g. the camel, see p. 61) are pronounced, as of the prohibited species by the text, which rigidly and unqualifiedly demands the two requisites mentioned. We further find, that by this requirement the law selects as the proper food of the Hebrews, those beasts *which possess the most perfect digestive apparatus*, and whose flesh, therefore, would be, according to principles laid down by eminent scientific authorities, of the most healthy description. By this dictum, also, the law includes as permitted, that large and most valuable class of domestic animals (the *Ruminantia*) which best minister to the dietary and other wants of men. As a further consequence we find that the remaining order of animals, which present, almost without exception, a catalogue of wild, carnivorous, rapacious, sanguinary and, but for their skins, chiefly useless, animals, whose digestive apparatus is of a plainer and less perfect character, and who possess, for the most part, a single stomach and claws to tear their prey,—that such form the prohibited class. And with respect to *birds* we find further that quite an identity exists in their chararacter, both with the permitted and prohibited; for the examination we have made shows us, that although there be some difference of opinion among Hebrew authorities themselves, respecting the enumerated species,* yet do they all agree, as do Christian critics, in referring an overwhelming proportion of them to the *Accipitres* or *Raptores*, which are birds of prey. Now, while these, like the beasts of prey, possess a less perfect digestive apparatus than that of the permitted birds, which include chiefly, though not exclusively, that valuable class known as the domestic,—theirs, as we have before shown, is of a more complicated and perfect character, establishing thus the referred to analogy in so far as concerns digestion, and, perhaps, the nature of their flesh. It is further established by the text objecting to those wild, carnivorous, rapacious and sanguinary birds possessing, like the prohibited beasts, a single stomach

---

* The number of species of birds known to naturalists is about 5000.

and claws to tear their prey. And it is further established in that there are instances of doubtful species among the enumerated birds, (e. g. the raven) just as there are among the enumerated beasts, which are, however, determined by the sacred text.* This premised, we may proceed to the consideration of the third point of inquiry, viz., the prohibition of the clean and unclean animals having reference to authority and reason.

As with the prohibition of blood, Hebrew authorities have assigned both religious or moral, and hygienic, reasons for the institution of such law; and as in the former case, we shall select the most valued of these authorities, and present them in an English dress to the reader, in conjunction with the illustrations afforded by other authors. We regard that most valuable and interesting—we believe, now very scarce, Spanish Jewish work, *Las Excelencias de los Hebreos*, as containing the most comprehensive digest of Jewish opinion on the matter. From it, therefore, shall we prefer to translate, commencing at the third division, (*Tercera Excelencia; Separados de todas las naciones*) at the 39th page.

"Three opinions are offered respecting this prohibition. The first is, that all the meats condemned by the law afford an objectionable and improper nourishment, deteriorating from the health and good temperament of the body, and embarassing the devotion of the soul. In this way speaks the great R. Moses, of Egypt (Maimonides, Mor. Neb. c. 3) when discoursing concerning the reasons of the precepts, referring, among other matters, to the swine, which he says is of a very humid nature, and that the principal cause of its prohibition is its extreme filthiness,—that had it been permitted to become a staple article of food, [its evils would have predominated over its advantages] for the streets and habitations would become as filthy as so many dirt receptacles, (muladares) as we find is the case with those uncleanly cities where the injurious practice of permitting these animals to congregate in public places [to collect their noisome food] obtains. [Could our author have seen some of the poorer Irish neighbourhoods and cabins, as we have seen them, both in Britain and America, presenting so many revolting sties where man and hog assist each other to engender and diffuse fever and pestilence, he would have found powerful and fearful testimony to the truth of the idea of which he writes.] The fat of the swine is, in itself, sufficient to impede the circulation, [and, we take leave to add, is one of the chief reasons why such fearfully vast quantities of intoxicating liquors are consumed in those countries

---

* See commentary of Abarbanel quoted on p. 54.